THE FOUR AGREEMENTS
COMPANION BOOK

Also by don Miguel Ruiz

THE FOUR AGREEMENTS
A Practical Guide to Personal Freedom

THE FOUR AGREEMENTS AUDIO
Read by actor Peter Coyote

THE MASTERY OF LOVE
A Practical Guide to the Art of Relationship

THE MASTERY OF LOVE AUDIO
Read by actors Jill Eikenberry and Michael Tucker

PRAYERS
A Communion with our Creator

THE VOICE OF KNOWLEDGE
A Practical Guide to Inner Peace

LOS CUATRO ACUERDOS
Una guía práctica para la libertad personal

CUADERNO DE TRABAJO DE LOS CUATRO ACUERDOS
Utiliza Los Cuatro Acuerdos para gobernar el sueño de tu vida

LA MAESTRÍA DEL AMOR
Una guía práctica para el arte de las relaciones

ORACIONES
Una comunión con nuestro Creador

Using The Four Agreements
to Master the Dream of Your Life

A
Toltec

THE FOUR AGREEMENTS
COMPANION BOOK

Wisdom
Book

DON MIGUEL RUIZ

WITH JANET MILLS

AMBER-ALLEN PUBLISHING
SAN RAFAEL, CALIFORNIA

Published by Amber-Allen Publishing, Inc.
P. O. Box 6657
San Rafael, CA 94903

Typography: Rick Gordon, Emerald Valley Graphics
Cover Art: Nicholas Wilton, Studio Zocolo
Cover Design: Michele Wetherbee
Cover Photo: Stephen Collector

Library of Congress Cataloging-in-Publication Data
Ruiz, Miguel, 1952– The four agreements companion book: using the four
agreements to master the dream of your life/don Miguel Ruiz.
p. cm. — (A Toltec wisdom book)
I. Conduct of life — Toltec philosophy — Miscellanea.
I. Title. II. Series: Ruiz, Miguel, 1952– Toltec wisdom book.
BJ1581.2 R85 2000   00-048089
299'.792 — dc21   CIP

ISBN 978-1-878424-48-8
Printed in Canada on acid-free paper
Distributed by Hay House, Inc.

12   14   16   18   20   19   17   15   13

DEDICATION

I believe in angels. Angel means messenger. I dedicate this book to the angels in human form that deliver a message of love instead of fear, superstition, and emotional poison.

To all the teachers from preschool to post-graduate school; to all who teach a better way of life. To all the artists, authors, leaders, movie directors, and media professionals who share themselves with generosity instead of selfishness to improve human lives. To all the parents who teach their children to be honest and compassionate. To anyone who loves and respects every human in the world.

Contents

CONTENTS

Practice Ideas

Mastering Awareness

Mastering Transformation

NOTE

If it has been some time since you last read *The Four Agreements*, you may want to refer to the Abbreviated Glossary on page 209, where a list of terms is provided for your convenience.

To avoid using the masculine gender exclusively when referring to both male and female readers, we have randomly used masculine and feminine pronouns throughout the book.

THE FOUR AGREEMENTS

1   BE IMPECCABLE WITH YOUR WORD

Speak with integrity. Say only what you mean. Avoid using the word to speak against yourself or to gossip about others. Use the power of your word in the direction of truth and love.

2   DON'T TAKE ANYTHING PERSONALLY

Nothing others do is because of you. What others say and do is a projection of their own reality, their own dream. When you are immune to the opinions and actions of others, you won't be the victim of needless suffering.

3   DON'T MAKE ASSUMPTIONS

Find the courage to ask questions and to express what you really want. Communicate with others as clearly as you can to avoid misunderstandings, sadness, and drama. With just this one agreement, you can completely transform your life.

4   ALWAYS DO YOUR BEST

Your best is going to change from moment to moment; it will be different when you are healthy as opposed to sick. Under any circumstance, simply do your best, and you will avoid self-judgment, self-abuse, and regret.

THE FOUR AGREEMENTS
COMPANION BOOK

in·teg·ri·ty (in teg′rə tē) 1. the quality or state of being complete; unbroken condition; wholeness; entirety 2. the quality or state of being unimpaired; perfect condition; soundness 3. the quality or state of being of sound moral principle; uprightness, honesty, and sincerity.

Introduction

Three Masteries, Four Agreements

The word is like a seed, and the human mind is so fertile, but only for those kinds of seeds it is prepared for.

THE FIRST TIME YOU READ *THE FOUR AGREEMENTS*, some part of you knows that you have heard these concepts before or have experienced them in your life, though perhaps not as simply.

In reading *The Four Agreements* you discover that humans create thousands of agreements based mainly on making assumptions and taking everything personally, and by doing this, we are using the power of our word against ourselves. We are using all the power of our creation to create a dream that sets us up to suffer for the rest of our lives.

The Four Agreements are a tool for transformation, leading you to stop judging, mainly yourself, and to start practicing another way of life. They lead you to stop the guilt, the shame, and the self-rejection; they help you break the agreements that limit the expression of your creativity, and replace them with new agreements that facilitate the expression of your love.

With *The Four Agreements,* my intention was to create a messenger that can enter the imagination of readers and change their point of view. If you have practiced these agreements, you already know what they can do. They have the capacity to go directly into your belief system, into those thousands of agreements you made with yourself, and create a doubt. And just like magic, because they *are* magic, the Four Agreements slowly free the faith that is trapped inside your belief system. Little by little, you recover your integrity, and the real you starts to awaken.

The Four Agreements are like a map that tells

you all the different ways to reach your destination. Their simplicity is what makes them so easy to use in so many directions. But the map is just one half. You are the other half. In any relationship, there are two halves. The book, the messenger, is one half of the relationship, but you are the other half, and that is the beauty of this relationship: your half.

If you have a goal and you use the messenger as your guide, you are going to reach your goal. With *The Four Agreements*, you can learn how to heal your emotional body. You can use it to change your belief system and create a brand new belief system. You can use it to heal your marriage, your relationships with your friends, and your relationships at work, and to improve your life in every way. But first, because it's a map, you have to start with awareness of where you are and where you want to be.

Thousands of years ago the Toltec created three masteries to guide us out of suffering and return us to our true nature: happiness, freedom, and love. The Toltec encouraged us to see ourselves with truth, and they created a mastery just for awareness. The first mastery, **the Mastery of Awareness,** is the first step toward personal freedom, because we cannot be free if we don't know what we are, where we are, or what kind of freedom we are looking for. In this mastery, we become aware of the fog that is in our mind. We become aware that we are dreaming all the time, and that everybody else is dreaming. The Mastery of Awareness can also be called the Mastery of Truth.

The second Toltec mastery, **the Mastery of Transformation,** shows us how to change the dream of our life. The goal of the second mastery is to put order into the chaos of the *mitote* — into all of the voices inside our mind — to face our fears, to transform our fears, and to get results. The result we want is the freedom to live our own life instead of the life of the Parasite or the belief system. The Mastery of Transformation is achieved by changing our agreements and reprogramming our own mind in our own way. The Four Agreements are a summary of the Mastery of Transformation.

The result of the first two masteries is a mind that

is Parasite-free, and that is the third mastery, **the Mastery of Love,** or **the Mastery of Intent.** From the Toltec point of view, love or intent is that part of life that makes the transformation of energy possible. It is Life itself; it is unconditional love. Everything is made with love because everything comes from God or Life. When we master love, we master the dream of our life, and when all three masteries are accomplished, we reclaim our divinity and become one with God. Then every action we take is an expression of the One Being. This is the goal of the Toltec.

For those of you who want to explore the third mastery, I have written a book called *The Mastery of Love*, which shows you what a dream based on love looks like. The Mastery of Love is the result of the first two masteries, and it offers a better way of living our life with love. But for now, the third mastery is not what we will focus on. The first two masteries are the subject of this book.

In the first part of this companion book, before we talk about applying the Four Agreements, the emphasis is on awareness. What do we want to be aware of? In Part One, we focus on three things:

1. *Human suffering begins with domestication.* When we are children, other people hook our attention and teach us to dream the way the society dreams. This is how our attention is used for the first time to create the first dream of our life.

2. *Humans are creators, but our power of creation is invested in our beliefs.* The power of our word, which is the same as our intent, our will, our faith, and our love, is trapped inside a rigid structure of beliefs. This leaves us with little power to change our dream.

3. *The function of the human mind is to dream, but we have learned to dream without awareness.* Once we are aware that we are dreaming, we awake from the dream and recover our power to change the dream whenever we choose.

When we discover that we have the power to create a dream of heaven, we want to change our dream, and the Four Agreements are the perfect tool for that.

In Part Two of this companion book, we explore several ways to master the art of dreaming:

4. *Using your will and attention for the second time.* In the dream of the second attention, you choose to believe what *you* want to believe, and that includes believing in yourself.

5. *Using the Four Agreements to change your actions—reactions.* Every choice you make has a consequence or result. When you change the action, you change the result, and you change the dream of your life.

6. *Using attach—detach to surrender to the angel of death.* The angel of death can teach you to live in the present moment instead of the past or the future. When your attention is in the present moment, you enjoy life more intensely because you are fully alive.

This companion book will give you more information about the first two masteries, but information is not enough. Information is merely the seed in your mind. What will really make the difference is action. If you practice the Four Agreements, you will master the Four Agreements. Eventually, after many repetitions, these agreements will become a habit, and you will see how your life is transformed.

There is a beautiful story about Jesus telling his disciples that his words are like seeds and he sends his seeds everywhere. Some seeds land on rock and never grow. Some seeds go into land that is fertile on the surface, but hard underneath; these seeds start sprouting, but soon die. Then there are the seeds that go into land that is very fertile, and they grow strong and become big trees. And you will know the tree by its fruit.

I love that metaphor. It is wonderful to see how many people who have practiced the Four Agreements have already grown into trees that bear fruit.

Just imagine if you could live in a society where the Four Agreements were a habit for everybody, where this habit was the way they expressed life. Imagine living in a society where everybody practiced love until they mastered love. It will happen; it is just a matter of time. There is already a new dream in this world that is ready to be dreamed by humans, Parasite-free.

The sun has already changed; the light has changed. We just need humans to dream the new dream.

By using the Four Agreements in our own life, we modify our personal dream, and soon our new dream will modify the outside dream. There is no need to actively try to modify the outside dream. This happens naturally as a result of our own transformation.

Deciding to focus on our own freedom isn't selfish; it is the greatest gift we can give to humanity.

PART ONE

Mastering Awareness

I

Domestication

Human suffering begins with domestication.

During the process of domestication, we form an image of perfection in order to try to be good enough. We create an image of how we should be in order to be accepted by everybody, but we don't fit this image.

ALL THE SUFFERING AND DRAMA IN YOUR LIFE IS the result of what you have learned. Whatever you learn is alive. The image that you have of yourself is alive, and it lives in your mind. That image is not you, but it will use everything it perceives to justify its own existence. It is not you, but it is eating you alive and destroying your happiness.

The voice of knowledge inside your mind controls the dream of your life. The Toltecs call it a *Parasite*; the Bible calls it *evil*. It is a living being that exists in your belief system, and lives by eating your faith, your intent, your happiness. What is sad is that you believe the knowledge *is* you; you believe *the image* is what you are. The program, or Parasite, is really the one who is living your life, not you. But this program was not there when you were born.

When you were born, your mind was completely innocent. You had no concepts about good or bad, right or wrong, beauty or ugliness; you had no concepts at all. You had no idea what it means to be a human, to be a man or to be a woman, but you saw other people outside of you, and you recognized them as your own kind.

When you are one, two, or three years old, you cannot see yourself. The only way to see yourself is to look at your image in a mirror, and other people act as that mirror. You don't know what you are, but your mother tells you what you are, and your father tells you what you are, and your brothers and sisters do the same thing. The other humans around you have the capacity to project an image onto you, which means they tell you what *they believe* you are.

What your mother tells you is not exactly what your father tells you that you are, or what your siblings, or the television, or the church, or the whole society tells you that you are. Every human in your life projects a completely different image onto you, and none of these images are accurate. What you believe you are is a distorted image of yourself that came from other people — from mirrors that always distort images. Because you cannot see yourself, you believe them and you agree with them. As soon as you agree, the image is programmed in your memory, and now you believe this is what you are.

What were the images others projected onto you? When you say, "I am smart, I am stupid, I am beautiful, I am ugly," it is really the program who says *I am.* These images are only knowledge or a lot of concepts, but they aren't you.

You perceive all the distorted images others create for you, and at a certain point you take all these images and try to make sense of them. You create another whole image of yourself, and project it to the outside world: I am good in school; I am bad in sports. Then you practice that image until you master it. And because people are projecting different images onto you, you are always asking them about yourself. You are asking for the projections to support what you already believe, to support the distorted images you have about yourself.

In the same way other people project their beliefs onto you, you agree, and they become yours. They teach you to judge the way they judge, to gossip the way they gossip, to create dramas the way they create dramas. You begin to play with all these concepts, all this knowledge, and that is how you learn to dream.

The Toltecs call this the *dream of the first attention* because it is the first time you used your attention to create a whole reality. And because your attention is hooked from the outside, your whole world is projected to the outside. You begin to search for yourself outside of you because you no longer trust who you are. You search for what you believe you don't have: justice, beauty, happiness, and love, when all of these were always inside you.

Can you see the beginning of all the suffering and drama in your life? You need a mirror in the world to see yourself, but there isn't a clear mirror to tell you what you are. So you agree with the image others create for you, but you are not that image. Of course you modify the image and you change it all the time, but where is the real you? It gets lost because there isn't a good mirror to reflect what you really are.

After years and years of trying to please other people's images of what you should be, after attempting different kinds of rebellion and trying to find who you really are, you finally give up and accept other people's images of what you are. But there is something inside you that longs to be free; it is always telling you, "This is not who I really am. This is not what I really want." You are not free to be who you really are because you are trapped by images of what you think you should be.

Your whole point of view of your whole reality is based on what you believe you are, but what you believe about yourself is just a concept. It is knowledge, but knowledge does not mean it is the truth. Knowledge only means it is what you know.

PRACTICE IDEA FOR MASTERING AWARENESS
THE IMAGE OF PERFECTION

The most important agreements are the ones you made with yourself. In these agreements you tell yourself who you are, what you feel, what you believe, and how to behave.

Are you aware of all the distorted images you have about yourself? What are the images that others projected onto you as a child? What did you *agree to believe* about yourself?

Consider any agreements that tell you what you can and cannot do, what you can and cannot be, and what you can and cannot have.

This practice idea will help you to become aware of the agreements you have made with yourself, and to recover the awareness of your authentic self. The objective is to become aware of any agreements that limit the expression of your creativity, your happiness, or your love.

Try to recall your earliest memories of what your mother, father, and closest family members told you about yourself. Then consider what other people outside your family projected onto you — friends, teachers, and other people who may have influenced you.

Pay attention to your emotional response to each question below. Which agreements come from fear, and which ones come from love? Record your thoughts and answers to these questions in a notebook or journal.

What were the images that others projected onto you?
 When I was a child, I was told that I was . . .
What limitations were you told you have?
 I was told that my limitations were . . .

When you were a child, what did others tell you about what it means to be a girl or a boy?

I was told that girls should always ...

I was told that boys should always ...

Did you fit the ideal image of what it meant to be a girl or a boy?

What do you believe today about being a woman or being a man?

I believe that a woman should always ...

I believe that a man should always ...

Make a list of all the qualities you were told you should have, both personal and physical.

I was told that I should be ...

Make a list of all the qualities you believe you have.

I believe I am ...

Make a list of all the qualities you believe *other* people think you have.

I believe that others think I am ...

Make a list of all the qualities you lack, but wish you had.

I wish I could be like this ...

Our image of perfection is the reason we reject ourselves; it is why we don't accept ourselves the way we are, and why we don't accept others the way they are.

Describe your image of perfection. What would you look like? What type of personality would you have?

My image of perfection is . . .

What would you have to change about yourself to live up to this image?

To achieve my image of perfection, I would have to . . .

Are you willing or able to make these changes? Why or why not?

Is it humanly possible for you to attain this image of perfection? Why or why not?

Does your image of perfection inspire you to do your best, or does it merely discourage you?

We judge others according to our image of perfection as well, and naturally they fall short of our expectations.

What is your image of perfection for other people in your life?

My image of perfection for my partner is . . .

My image of perfection for my child is . . .

My image of perfection for my parents is . . .
My image of perfection for my best friend is . . .
My image of perfection for my co-workers is . . .
My image of perfection for my boss is . . .

We know we are not what we believe we are supposed to be and so we feel false, frustrated, and dishonest. We try to hide ourselves, and we pretend to be what we are not. The result is that we feel unauthentic and wear social masks to keep others from noticing this.

What social masks do you wear around others?
My social masks are . . .

Do you wear these masks because you are afraid of other people's judgments?
I wear these masks because . . .

What would happen if you took the masks off?
If I take the masks off . . .

What would it be like to express who you really are?
If I expressed who I really am . . .

After domestication it is no longer about being good enough for anybody else. We are not good enough for ourselves because we don't fit with our own image of perfection.

On a scale of one to ten, with number one being the distorted images you agreed with, and number ten being your authentic self, where do you presently reside on this scale?

On the authenticity scale, I reside at number:

1...2...3...4...5...6...7...8...9...10

List at least four new agreements you can make with yourself that will honor who you really are.

I intend to honor my authentic self by ...

Make a commitment to move a step closer toward your authentic self by practicing your four new agreements.

THE BOOK OF LAW

Without question, whatever is in that Book of Law, is our truth. We base all of our judgments according to the Book of Law, even if these judgments go against our own inner nature.

One of the biggest mystery schools in the world, Christianity, tells the story about Adam and Eve who lived in paradise, Parasite-free. They perceived everything with their awareness, and they had a beautiful dream, but they didn't have knowledge.

In the middle of the garden was the Tree of Knowledge, and God warned Adam and Eve not to eat the fruit from this tree. Do you remember who lives in that tree? The evil serpent lives there. Well, I like to change the name of the serpent, the devil, to the *Parasite*. The Parasite lives in the fruit of the Tree of Knowledge, and it's just like the little worm you sometimes see inside an apple. If you eat the apple, you eat the Parasite. The serpent or evil goes into your mind through knowledge contaminated by the Parasite.

Humans accumulate a lot of knowledge, and 95 percent of that knowledge is not true. Instead of using knowledge as a tool for communication, we become puppets of knowledge. We give life to that knowledge, and that knowledge begins to create a lot of drama and suffering because it isn't based on truth.

Six or seven hundred years ago everybody knew that the earth was flat. This didn't mean that it was true; but they *knew*, and they *believed*, and for them the earth was flat. When they unlearned that knowledge, their perception changed, the concept changed, and now we know that the earth is round. This kind of concept is harmless really, but other concepts are deadly — especially the concepts that try to rule people's lives.

As children, we never chose what to believe or not to believe. We didn't choose our religion or moral values, or any concept at all. But we agreed with these beliefs, and once we agreed, it was stored in our memory. The outside dream hooked our attention and put knowledge inside us via other humans — via our parents, our teachers, our church, our society. This knowledge sets us up to be slaves of the dream of the planet.

Knowledge itself isn't good or bad or right or wrong; knowledge is just a program. It is nothing but concepts. But the Parasite that goes with knowledge is evil — it is alive. That Parasite grows in your mind and takes control of the mind. Once that Parasite takes control of your mind, the real you is dead. You are not alive; there is something else that is living your life.

It is not you because the real you is not evil; the real you is not self-destructive.

We eat knowledge, ingest the Parasite, and get sick from what we eat. This is what happened to all of us. When we understand that evil is nothing but a disease of the human mind, we understand why human societies are the way they are, why there is all the injustice, violence, and war. We have ingested Parasites in the form of beliefs, in the form of concepts, in the form of distorted images. All of the personal drama that we experience — all the emotions that burn us up, that lead us into self-destruction, into addictions, into lies, into dogmas and fanaticism — are the result of our beliefs, the result of a program.

If we can see that we get sick by eating knowledge, then using logic, how can we heal ourselves? What happens when we eat food that is contaminated and we don't feel well? If we throw up and get rid of the poison, we are going to feel better. Well, if we get rid of the knowledge that harms us, guess who goes out with that knowledge? Once we take the Parasite out of the mind, the mind will heal and will function much better.

The story of Adam and Eve tells us what happened, and in all the traditions around the world, in one way or another, they have come to the same conclusion. The whole dream of the planet is not real; it is not true. When you awake from that dream and are aware of what is going on in people's minds, you see Parasites everywhere in everyone. You see all the emotional poison coming out through those Parasites. By being aware, you see that wherever you go, people react the same way that you react; they have the same fears, the same jealousy, the same anger, the same sorrows. You can see yourself in each one of them, and they mirror your projections, but we don't have to judge it as good or bad or right or wrong; it is just the way it is.

To be aware of what happened with our mind and with the whole humanity is what the Toltec call the Mastery of Awareness. Awareness means to open your eyes to see the truth, and no longer to be blind. We are born with awareness, but we accumulate knowledge and we practice not being aware; we learn to deny what we perceive. We are born without knowledge, of course, but we accumulate knowledge when we are domesticated. That knowledge is like a wall of fog that doesn't allow us to perceive what really is; it keeps us from having awareness.

The challenge is to maintain our awareness in the midst of that fog. More than that, to *shift* the knowledge, lift the fog, and recover our awareness. If we can practice being aware all the time, just the awareness will change our whole reality. When we master awareness, we almost master the dream.

There is a movie called *The Crucible* that portrays how the evil serpent enters people's minds through knowledge. In the movie, a real man of knowledge came to town carting several large books. He had spent all his life learning about witchcraft, and was full of that knowledge. The church knew there were witches among them, and they were determined to clean up the town. They judged the whole town based on those books, and many people were killed. One little girl had the power to condemn whomever she wanted to condemn by lying. If she said, "I see the devil in that person," they went to trial, were judged and found guilty, and they were killed. The whole town was possessed by fear, but where was the evil? Was it in those people who were killed? No, the evil was in those books of knowledge; it was in that man who was determined to apply the law in the name of that knowledge.

Well, each of us has the same kind of book in our head. We have our own book of knowledge, our own *Book of Law*, and we use that book to judge ourselves, to find ourselves guilty, and to punish ourselves. Many times we even deny ourselves the right to be alive. Again, it is important to understand that our mind is infested with a lot of little Parasites or concepts that other people put in our mind. Together those Parasites create one big Parasite, and they stay in our mind by agreement.

The belief that you are not good enough is one of the little Parasites in your mind. It is evil because it is destroying you. It causes suffering because it limits your life, it limits your creativity and your happiness. The belief that nobody likes you, the belief that you are not worthy of love or happiness, the belief that you are always right — these beliefs are not true, and they lead you into self-destruction. By always being right, for example, you have to make someone else wrong. By making someone else wrong, you create an enemy and then you are hurting yourself because sooner or later that enemy will go against you.

All these concepts are alive and they work together, but they need your mind, they need your dream, they need your emotions to be alive. They only live because you *believe* them. These Parasites are what the old religions called gods or demons. They have many names, but they are truly alive, and they are in control of the human mind.

Every concept, every belief in your mind has its own personality that wants to express itself. You have millions of voices in your head, a whole society inside your mind, and just like a democracy, what the majority wants is the way you live your life. That inner society is governed by rules that dictate the way your life should be, the way each part of you has to behave. The whole dream of your life is based on the rules in your Book of Law, and whatever happens in your life will be interpreted according to that Book of Law.

And there are two other parts that live in your mind: One is the *Judge*, and the other is the *Victim*. The Judge is doing its job perfectly. Its job is to judge, and it uses the Book of Law to judge everything. Every action and reaction lives under the tyranny of the Judge. The part of you that receives the judgment, or sometimes the reward, is the Victim. Whether the Victim receives a reward or a punishment will depend on whether or not you follow the Book of Law.

The Judge and the Victim have no doubt that the Book of Law is the supreme truth and nothing but the truth. They rule the dream in the Book of Law without any doubt, which means they rule with faith. That is how you live your life, but the big question is this: Is there justice in that system? In *The Four Agreements* we have already found that there is no justice in that system. All the suffering of humanity is in that Book of Law, that book of knowledge, because it isn't based on truth. Again, more than 90 percent of that knowledge is not true, but for the Judge and the Victim, it is absolutely true.

....

PRACTICE IDEA FOR MASTERING AWARENESS
THE BOOK OF LAW

....

One by one, all these agreements go into the Book of Law, and these agreements rule our dream.

Are you aware of the agreements that govern your life? What does your Book of Law say about how you should treat yourself? What does it say about how you should relate with other people, with other forms of life, with God? Does your Book of Law give you the freedom to be who you really are? Does it give you the right to be happy, the right to express your creativity, the right to be generously rewarded for the gifts and talents you share with others?

Keep a separate journal for recording all the agreements you have made in your life. Label this journal "The Book of Law," and make a commitment to record every law, every rule, every agreement or belief that you become aware of for at least one full year. Keep your Book of Law within easy reach so you don't forget!

Below are some suggestions for chapter headings and subtopics in your Book of Law. This is *your* Book of Law, so feel free to make up your own headings, to use words and descriptions that you personally relate to.

Personal Agreements: Your Body and Your Self
    Personal Appearance
    Health and Diet
    Masculinity and Femininity

Social Agreements: Family and Friends
    Love and Sex
    Marriage and Family
    Friendship and Social Interactions

Spiritual Agreements: Life and God
    Religion and Spirituality
    Death and Loss
    Nature, Animals, and All Forms of Life

Financial Agreements: Work and Career
    Your Unique Skills and Talents
    Money and Financial Matters
    Success and Failure

After you have entered the headings for your Book of Law, consider what you were programmed to believe about each of these areas of your life. What did you learn about yourself, about others, about work, about life? One way to get started is to ask "good or bad" or "right or wrong" questions for each topic within a chapter. For example:

What is good or bad, or right or wrong, about . . .
    My personal appearance?
    My personality?
    Being a woman or being a man?
    Being married?
    Having children?
    Making money?

Being successful?

My religion and my spirituality?

My job and profession?

Consider how you were domesticated as a very young child.

How did other people hook your attention?

How were you rewarded?

How were you punished?

What did you do to hook the attention of other people?

What did you do to avoid being punished?

What did you do to get the reward?

List four of the most important values you learned from:

Parents, siblings, and other family members

School or church

Baby-sitters, or other influential adults

Friends and acquaintances

Society at large

Do you agree with each of these values?

As a child, were you punished if you didn't honor these values?

As an adult, do you punish yourself for failing to honor them?

List some of the self-abusive agreements you have made with yourself.

List some of the self-nurturing, self-loving agreements you have made with yourself.

As you become aware of any other agreements you have made, record them in your Book of Law.

THE JUDGE

The inner Judge uses what is in our Book of Law to judge everything we do and don't do, everything we think and don't think, and everything we feel and don't feel. Everything lives under the tyranny of this Judge.

Are you aware of the Judge inside your mind, the "voice of knowledge" that judges everything and everyone?

Make a list of every person in your life, including yourself. Consider how each person conducts his or her life in each category in your Book of Law. Briefly describe your judgments about each person. How do you feel about the way each person lives his or her life, including you? What do you admire about yourself and every other person on your list. What do you dislike or even despise?

Remember: We make the assumption that other people judge us the way we judge ourselves, but this isn't true. Other people judge us according to their own Book of Law; they live in a completely different dream. And we judge other people the way we judge ourselves because all of our judgments come from the supreme truth in our Book of Law.

How do you judge yourself?

> I am a bad person because . . .
>
> I should be ashamed of myself because . . .
>
> I am guilty of . . .
>
> I am so stupid whenever I . . .

How do you judge others?

> That person is bad because . . .
>
> That person should be ashamed of herself because . . .
>
> That person is guilty of . . .
>
> I think it's really stupid when someone . . .

List four mistakes you have made in your life.

> How do you punish yourself?
>
> How do you abuse yourself?
>
> How many times have you paid for each mistake?
>
> Do you abuse your physical body?

List four mistakes other people have made that you cannot forgive.

How do you punish others?

How do you abuse others?

How many times have you made each person pay for his or her mistake?

Do you abuse other people physically?

List four things you have accomplished that made you proud of yourself.

How did you reward yourself?

List four things others have accomplished that made you proud of them.

How did you reward them?

Now that you are more aware of your Judge, describe in detail what your Judge is like and how it uses the Book of Law to rule your life. Is your Judge ever fair and forgiving, or is it always harsh and unforgiving?

Consider giving your Judge a more personal or descriptive name so you can easily identify whose voice is talking inside your head.

YOUR ANSWER TO THE JUDGE

The next time the voice of the Judge is judging you or anyone else, you now have four answers to give the Judge. You can decide which answer is most appropriate for the situation. Get a bright piece of paper and black marking pen, and create a note to remind yourself of these answers. Then post the note where you will see it every day.

Big deal.
Who cares?
So what?
Why not?

And if none of these answers seem to satisfy your Judge, then remember this: It doesn't matter.

THE VICTIM

The Victim carries the blame, the guilt, and the shame. It is the part of us that says, "Poor me, I'm not good enough, I'm not intelligent enough, I'm not attractive enough, I'm not worthy of love. . . ."

Are you aware of the Victim inside your mind that receives the judgments, carries the blame, the guilt, and the shame?

The Victim is that part of you that feels helpless, hopeless, or powerless.

> What makes you feel ashamed of yourself?
> What makes you feel guilty?
> What makes you feel helpless or victimized?
> When do you feel unworthy of love?
> When do you feel regret or sadness?
> When do you feel betrayed?

Complete the following sentences:

> I am to blame for being . . .
> I don't deserve to have . . .
> I can't do what I really want to do because . . .
> I am powerless when it comes to . . .
> Poor me, I am not good enough to . . .
> Poor me, I am not intelligent enough to . . .
> Poor me, I am never going to be . . .
> Poor me, I am never going to have . . .
> I am unworthy of self-love because . . .
> I am unworthy of self-respect because . . .
> I am unworthy of being too happy because . . .
> I am unworthy of financial abundance because . . .

Look at your answers to the statements above, and ask your heart, not your Parasite, whether each statement is true or false. Here's a hint to let you know when you are telling yourself a lie: Any belief that generates fear or feelings of unworthiness is false; it's a lie. The Parasite thrives on the emotions that come from fear, suffering, and drama. Our authentic self would never abuse us; it comes from love.

Describe in detail what your Victim is like. When does it believe the Judge? Why does it believe the Judge? Consider giving your Victim a personal name so you can identify its voice in your head.

On a scale of one to ten, with number one being a life that is governed by the Parasite (the Judge, the Victim, and the Book of Law), and number ten being a life completely free of the Parasite, where do you presently live your life?

On the Parasite scale, I live my life at number:

1 . . . 2 . . . 3 . . . 4 . . . 5 . . . 6 . . . 7 . . . 8 . . . 9 . . . 10

Spend the next fifteen minutes considering what it would be like to live your life without the Judge and the Victim. Imagine if you could take back the power you gave to the Judge years ago, and rule your life based on principles of love, joy, and freedom. Imagine if your Victim was transformed from "poor me" to an empowered person who refuses to be abused one minute longer.

Imagine what your life would be like if your personal code of conduct was based on the Four Agreements. When you try to imagine these possibilities, do you find yourself meeting resistance?

Complete the following sentences:
I cannot live my life without the Judge because . . .
I cannot live my life without the Victim because . . .
I cannot rule my life the way I really want to because . . .
I cannot live my life by the Four Agreements because . . .

What kind of excuses does your Parasite give you? Write these down so you can respond to them with truth instead of lies. As you read your answers to each of the above sentences, counter each excuse with a reason why it *would* be possible for you to do it. Come up with at least one answer to each statement that completely refutes the excuse. As you counter each excuse, imagine yourself moving up the scale toward a life that is Parasite-free.

Keep answering your excuses, and continue to imagine yourself moving up the scale until you reach the number ten. At this point, you no longer have any doubt that you can accomplish what you want. You have recovered your faith from the belief system, and your faith is 100 percent.

Here is an example:
I cannot live my life without the Judge because . . .

1. I would be completely irresponsible and out of control.
2. I would do bad things.
3. I would be lazy and never get anything done.

Your answers to the above statements might be:

1. I would never be irresponsible or out of control. I am a responsible person and if I praised myself more, and judged myself less, I would be happier and more capable of assuming responsibility.

2. I would never do anything bad. In fact, if the Judge wasn't always judging me, I would do greater things than I do now. If I accepted myself without judgment, I would accept others without judgment.

3. I am not a lazy person. Perhaps I would take it easy for a while, but then I would enjoy doing what I need to do and would accomplish even more without the Judge always criticizing me.

Complete your response to each limiting belief, then take another look at the Parasite scale and ask yourself where your life resides. Were you able to move your position a step closer to number ten? If not, why not? What will it take for you to reclaim your personal freedom?

This practice idea can be used for almost any area of your life in which you find yourself challenged. Start by making a statement about something you want, but fear you will not get. Consider all the reasons why you cannot have what you want. Then come up with a statement that completely negates each of these excuses. Imagine each excuse as a physical object that is standing in the way of your goal. Imagine yourself moving up the scale as you remove each obstacle from your path.

Keep working with both lists until you reach the point where your faith is completely invested in your desire instead of your doubt. At this point, you will be at number ten on the scale.

The agreements that come from fear require us to expend a lot of energy, but the agreements that come from love help us to conserve energy and even gain extra energy.

You should now be aware of some of the judgments, beliefs, and agreements in your Book of Law. The next step is to challenge the agreements in your Book of Law. Go through your Book of Law and ask yourself these questions:

Which of these agreements lift me up and give me joy?
Which of these agreements bring me down?
Which of these agreements are based on truth?
Which of these agreements are lies?

Identify each limiting, fear-based agreement, and write a new agreement based on truth and self-love to replace it. Begin each week with one agreement that seems the easiest to break. Focus your attention on that agreement until you can break that agreement and adopt the new one in its place.

Practice your new agreement until it becomes a habit. As you break each agreement, your enthusiasm and self-respect will continue to grow until you recover enough power to break all of the agreements that limit your freedom and happiness.

2

The Power of the Word

**Humans are creators, but our power of creation
is invested in our beliefs.**

*Through the word, you express your creative power. It is through
the word that you manifest everything. Regardless of what language
you speak, your intent manifests through the word.*

OUR POWER OF CREATION IS THE WORD. THE WORD
is the most powerful tool that humans possess. It is the
tool of magic.

The word creates the light, and because light is the
messenger of Life, the word *is* Life or God. The Gospel
of John in the Bible expresses the power of the word
quite clearly: "In the beginning was the word, and the

word was with God, and the word is God." Regardless of the language we speak, our *intent* manifests through the word. Through the word we manifest everything; we express our will, our intent, our love, and our faith, which are all the same thing.

Let's consider what it means to have faith. Whoever masters faith, masters the dream. Why? Because faith is the impeccability of the word. To have faith is to believe 100 percent without a doubt. Faith is how the word is manifested; it is how we guide our intent. To have great faith is to have great power because our intent, our will, is undivided. When our word isn't dissipated by doubt, the power of our word is even stronger.

The great leaders of humanity have a lot of personal power because they have great faith. But their faith comes from the heart, not the head. Their faith comes from love instead of fear, and from wisdom instead of knowledge. The kind of faith that comes from the head is blind faith because it comes from knowledge, from false beliefs, from fear. Blind faith is a faith that leads to fanaticism and dogmatism, which explains all the religious wars, all the fear that other people don't believe what we believe. Blind faith is a faith that we have to defend and impose on other people in order to feel validated and safe.

Humans are powerful creators. We are born with all the faith of the universe, and everything we create is based on faith. That faith is really our personal power, but what has happened with our faith? We invest all our faith in our beliefs and agreements, and we are left with little power to change our lives.

Imagine that every agreement is just like a brick. Humans create an entire structure out of bricks, and we glue it together with our faith. We believe without a doubt in all the knowledge inside that structure. Our faith gets trapped inside that structure because we put our faith in each agreement. It's not important if it is or isn't true; we believe it, and for us it is true.

All of our power of creation is invested in our belief, and because we believe it, that's the way it is. If we believe our knowledge, whatever we perceive will be filtered to make it fit into that knowledge. We create a personal dream that justifies the knowledge, and the outside dream proves to us that what we believe is true. The outside dream reflects our personal dream; it will justify every belief.

During all the education we receive, which means all the knowledge that is programmed in our mind, we create the concept of the *I am*. Everything we believe we are, everything we know about how to be a human is the *I am*. The Toltec call this *the human form*. We are not talking about the physical body, but about our own dream. When we say, "I am a man; I am a woman; I am a human, and this is my whole reality," everything is judged by that knowledge, and of course, the dream becomes hell. That is the drama of humanity.

The dream of our life is so limited because we take all the power of our creation and put it in a little box, and with all our power we seal the box. And we live inside the box, trapped inside that little box. Well, that little box is the human form. It is our creation, and all our will is invested in that *I am*.

Your faith is so strong that when you believe "I am never going to be this," *thy will be done,* you are never going to be that. If you believe "I cannot do it," *thy will be done,* you cannot do it. Whatever you believe, you put your faith in that belief, and your faith will make it true.

The power of our word is behind every agreement we make. To break an agreement, we need to have at least the same amount of power we used to make the agreement, but we find that we no longer have enough power to break an agreement just because we decide to. The classic example of this is the agreement to smoke. Our reasoning mind can understand that it's not good for us to smoke, and we decide not to smoke anymore. Our mind says, "I will not smoke anymore because it's not good for me." Then we open the package, light a cigarette, and keep smoking. We don't want to smoke and we try not to smoke, but we still smoke! The temptation to smoke is stronger than our will; or we can say our will and our faith are not yet strong enough to keep our word.

Why don't we have enough power to break our agreements? Imagine that we had one hundred units of power, and we put four units of power into the agreement to smoke. In theory, we need at least four units of power to break this agreement. But the problem is that the other ninety-six units of power are already being used to keep all the agreements of our whole reality alive. Then the day we decide not to smoke anymore, we don't have enough power to change the agreement. All of our power has been taken.

What happened to the other ninety-six units of power? Let's look at the way we spend energy. In *The Four Agreements*, we talked about this example: Imagine you awake one morning with a lot of energy. You can hardly wait to do a lot of things. You go to eat your breakfast, and for whatever reason, you have a big fight with your spouse. All these angry words are said, all these painful emotions come out, and after the fight, all you want to do is go to bed and sleep. The fight drains all your energy.

To save energy you need to change your routines, change those agreements, and no longer react with those emotions. If your spouse wants to fight, and you don't fight, then you still have that energy. You just eat your breakfast quickly, and leave the room. It's up to you whether you will allow yourself to spend all your energy on your emotions. You don't have to be the victim of your emotions.

The emotions that drain you are the emotions that come from fear; the emotions that give you more energy are those that come from love.

Most people spend all their energy on personal importance, on defending their image, on defending their opinions and what they believe. They spend a lot of energy trying to be right and making everybody else wrong. This nonsense behavior is funny when you see it from the outside, but it becomes a big drama when you are in the middle of it. That drama drains our energy. To believe what we believe, to keep all these agreements alive, we have no energy left. Our power of creation, the word, is dissipated by the big *mitote* in our mind, by all those conflicting agreements we create. The result is that we feel powerless.

As we have said, the Book of Law, even though it isn't physical, creates a strong and rigid structure made by agreements, and we call it a belief system. From a single letter to a whole ideology, everything we believe goes into that structure, and it is almost as rigid as our physical body. The agreements we make control our whole dream, and the structure is so strong that it looks like it's impossible to break.

Well, what happens if we start taking bricks from that structure? At a certain point the whole edifice will collapse. And that is what happens when we practice the Four Agreements. The Book of Law starts falling apart little by little, and at a certain point, it is no longer strong enough to control the dream of our life. The belief structure collapses, and we lose the human form, the *I am.*

When that happens, the dream of our life looks like chaos. It looks like chaos because it *is* chaos. When we lose the human form, the old order no longer exists, the old dream doesn't govern our life anymore. Our emotions get stronger, the poison starts coming out, and it's a great opportunity for cleansing. Even though it is chaos, we now have a chance to rewrite the Book of Law and create new agreements with knowledge.

If we keep practicing the Four Agreements, we are going to break all those images we created for ourselves, all those images that were projected onto us by our mother and father, our brothers and sisters, our friends, society, everybody. Of course, for years we have practiced all those images, we create attachments, and those attachments come from our faith. We are so attached to our images, to our beliefs, that if something challenges our beliefs or takes them away from us, it hurts. And because it hurts, even if those beliefs create a life of drama and emotional pain, we resist the change.

That is why breaking the belief structure and losing the human form should be gradual, not fast. In certain cases it can happen fast, but to take off your social masks and lose your images can create a strong emotional reaction. In the end, of course, the truth will set you free, but the truth is painful to discover because most of your attachments and resistance to life are not based on truth, but on lies.

Losing the human form can be emotionally painful because you are going against your own beliefs. The Judge and the Victim know you very well and will use anything they can to go against *you*. If you have a strong desire to change your Book of Law, it is going to happen, but you cannot expect the change to come without crisis. You are breaking your beliefs, your awareness is expanding, and you are learning to dream in your own way. You have to go step-by-step; you cannot expect the transformation to happen from one moment to another. In theory, of course, anything is possible. Maybe it is possible to jump from elementary school to college, but you cannot expect that at all. If you lose the human form, then even more things are possible. As you break all those beliefs that tell you what isn't possible, incredible things start happening to you because you don't limit yourself anymore.

Even though you are different, people assume you are the same; they hardly notice the change unless you express yourself. But at a certain point, you no longer play their game. You don't take on their addictions, and you don't join in their gossiping. You no longer care so much about their drama, about their anger, their jealousy, because you know they are dreaming. And you know they don't mean it when they tell you something unkind.

You love and respect yourself so much that you don't allow other people to disrespect you. You put boundaries on their wounds, not because you want to avoid them, but because you don't allow that poison to come to you. You don't judge other people, but you don't accept their poison because accepting their poison is going against yourself.

Once you lose the human form, you find out that you don't know what you are, and you no longer care about what you are. When you break the image of what it means to be a human, you are no better than a rock, but then, nobody is better than you either. In this society, to be human means to be at the top of evolution on this planet, to be superior to other kinds of life in this world; to be superior to dogs, cats, plants, and rocks. But when you reach a certain level of awareness in your mind, you are no longer human from that point of view. To be human is no longer important, because you see life from a whole new perspective. You are the same as everything else that exists in the universe; you come from the same source, you are made of the same light. And if you are no better than anyone, and no one is better than you, then where is personal importance?

The Mastery of Transformation is the process of unlearning what you have already learned. If you learn by making agreements, you unlearn by breaking agreements. When you unlearn, that knowledge is no longer in your mind. If that knowledge is no longer in your mind, the voice of knowledge, the Parasite, is no longer in your mind either.

By applying the Four Agreements you are going to free your faith, free your word, and unlearn the knowledge. It is best to start by breaking agreements that are very small and require less power. As those smaller agreements are broken, your personal power will increase until you reach a point when you can finally face the big demons in your mind.

Every time you break an agreement, the power of your faith that you invested in that agreement comes back to you. You no longer need to spend your power to keep that agreement alive. You recover your personal power, your will becomes stronger, and this gives you the power to change another agreement, and another, and another.

As you keep applying the Four Agreements, you discover something very interesting: Most of the small agreements are broken almost immediately. You start seeing results right away, and your personal power increases right away. Every time you read *The Four Agreements* again, you see how you used the word against yourself again, you see why you don't need to take anything personally or make assumptions again. Then you can face the bigger agreements, and start a cycle of rebuilding your personal power. Every time you read the book, your will grows stronger because you recover more and more of your integrity. You become more and more of who you really are because you are breaking the domestication.

Once your Book of Law is broken and you lose the human form, knowledge and the Book of Law is no longer the big tyrant in your life. Knowledge is still there, but it doesn't have the order that it did before. The structure is broken, but now you are in a position to choose a new structure.

You no longer believe in all your knowledge, and your relationship with knowledge changes completely. Before, knowledge had you enslaved inside that little box; it controlled your life. Now, *you* have power over knowledge. You still use knowledge as a tool of communication, but knowledge no longer abuses you.

Understanding how the structure of our dream is made, gives us an opportunity to challenge our beliefs, and change our dream. But awareness is always the first step toward our freedom. Without awareness there is no way out of the structure.

....

PRACTICE IDEA FOR MASTERING AWARENESS
THE POWER OF THE WORD

....

The word is not just a sound or a written symbol. The word is a force; it is the power you have to express and communicate, to think, and thereby to create the events in your life.

Are you aware of the power of your word? Take a moment to consider the power of certain words you were told as a child. Can you remember a time when someone you know "put a spell on you" with the power of his word? How have these words affected your life? Now think of a more recent time when you or someone you know used the power of her word with the intent to spread emotional poison. You must understand what the word *is* and what the word *does*. The word is a vibration of sound that has the tendency to manifest its physical equivalent. And just as a seed carries the potential to propagate a forest, the word carries the potential to take root in your mind and spontaneously generate thought forms of a similar vibration. Eventually, your personal dream will reflect the type of seeds that have rooted in your mind.

CONTEMPLATE THE POWER OF THE WORD

Spend the next twenty minutes considering the power of the word. If you have a dictionary or thesaurus, look up the origin and meaning of your favorite words. Make a list of these, and then ask yourself what you like about their sound and their meaning. Notice how different words can affect your emotions, how some lift you up and others bring you down. Ask yourself this question again and again: What is a word? Contemplate this question until you are satisfied that you can feel the power that lies within the word.

Once you are truly aware of the power of the word, you will find it easier to choose your words carefully, to speak with integrity, and to say only what you mean.

BEWARE OF COMMON PHRASES AND CULTURAL EXPRESSIONS

Every culture has common phrases, sayings, and expressions that people learn early on and then mindlessly repeat. Since habitual thoughts and words tend to manifest in physical form, do we really want to reinforce these messages? Identify four or more things you hear people say repeatedly that go against themselves. Here are some examples:

I'm getting too old for this.

I'm sick and tired of doing that.

I'm dying to . . .

I can't afford to . . .

Identify four or more things people mindlessly tell others that go against themselves. Some examples are:

You're a pain in the neck (or elsewhere).

I'm going to kill you.

Why don't you drop dead?

I wish you would get lost.

Do you also have the habit of saying these things? Do you curse yourself or other people when you're feeling frustrated or angry? Look at your lists and make a commitment to clean up your speech. Garbage in, garbage out. Poison in, poison out. Lies in, lies out. Truth in, truth out. Love in, love out. Like attracts like when it comes to the word.

You can measure the impeccability of your word by your level of self-love. How much you love yourself and how you feel about yourself are directly proportionate to the quality and integrity of your word.

Self-love begins with self-respect

Imagine how you would speak to someone whom you love and respect immensely. If you have a pet dog or cat that you love and adore, how do you speak to your animal friend? Now consider how you speak to yourself. What do you say to yourself every day when you look in the mirror, when you are bathing or dressing or going about your day? If you speak to yourself in a critical, judgmental way, it's because you have learned to do this from others. You *agreed* to treat yourself this way, then you practiced this habit until you mastered it.

Now that you are aware of the agreement, you can choose to break it by saying: "I no longer agree to treat myself with disrespect. Every time a self-critical thought comes to mind, I will forgive the Judge and follow this comment with words of praise, self-acceptance, and love."

Make a list of at least four things you say to yourself *about yourself* every day. Then review your list and decide whether these words are kind, respectful, and loving. Treat yourself as you would treat a queen or king, an innocent child, or your favorite pet. Choose to be impeccable with your word. Self-love begins with self-respect.

THE POWER OF THE WORD

When you become impeccable with your word, your mind is no longer fertile ground for words that come from black magic. Instead, it is fertile for the words that come from love.

PUT AN END TO GOSSIP

Are you aware of the destructive power of gossip? Gossip is black magic because it spreads emotional poison, perpetuates fear, and keeps others down. Consider the harm that has been done by gossiping about yourself or about others.

At first it may be difficult to avoid gossip entirely, but eventually you will see how breaking the agreement to gossip will transform your life. Are you ready to make a new agreement about the way you communicate with others?

Take note of when, where, and with whom you engage in gossip.

Do you also gossip about yourself?

How does gossip make you feel about yourself?

Do you find yourself feeling guilty for something you have said?

How does gossip affect your relationships with other people?

List four reasons you enjoy gossiping about yourself or about others.

List four compelling reasons to put an end to gossip.

List four times when gossiping caused needless suffering for you or someone you know.

List four steps you can take to avoid gossiping or to discourage others around you from gossiping (such as changing the subject, saying something positive, walking away, or remaining silent).

Break the agreement to gossip, and make a new agreement to be impeccable with your word.

Pay attention to your conversation with others. Stay aware and stay awake. Refuse to engage in gossip.

Practice avoiding gossip for one day, then one week, then two weeks, then an entire month.

Keep practicing until you break the habit of gossiping and establish a new habit of sharing truth and love.

When we believe something, we assume we are right about it to the point that we will destroy relationships in order to defend our position.

The Power of the Word

Let go of the need to defend your opinions and always be right

Complete the following sentences:

I know that I'm right because . . .

Other people are usually wrong because . . .

I need to prove that I'm right because . . .

It's important to defend my opinions and my point of view because . . .

Your opinion is nothing but your point of view. It is not necessarily true.

List four times when defending your opinion caused emotional drama in your relationships with others.

List four compelling reasons not to defend your opinions or always be right.

Make a commitment to spend one hour, then four hours, then one day, then one week at a time without defending your opinions.

Being impeccable with your word is the correct use of your energy; it means to use your energy in the direction of truth and love for yourself.

USE THE POWER OF YOUR WORD IN THE DIRECTION
OF TRUTH AND LOVE

Complete the following sentences:

I am not impeccable with my word when I . . .

I could be impeccable with my word by . . .

I can use the power of my word in the direction of truth by . . .

I can use the word to share my love by . . .

List four times when misuse of your word caused needless suffering for you or someone you know.

List four compelling reasons to be impeccable with your word.

Make a new agreement with yourself to be impeccable with your word, and write this agreement on paper.

Nurture your seeds of love by reading your written agreement every day for at least four weeks or until you firmly establish the habit of being impeccable with your word.

Use the word to share your love. When you are impeccable with your word, you feel good; you feel happy and at peace.

Symbolize the power of your word

Select an object to symbolize the power of your word, and to remind you to *be impeccable with your word.* Be sure to place the object where you will see it every day: on your dresser, in your car, on your desk, in your kitchen. It's important that the symbol be meaningful to you. Here are some suggestions:

Imagine the word as a seed with the potential to produce an entire field or forest of its own kind. Some seeds will create a beautiful field of flowers or an enchanted forest of trees; others will create a field of weeds and thistles. (Any seed such as an acorn can function as your symbol.)

Imagine the word as a sword with two edges. One edge represents "truth" with the power to create a dream of heaven; the other edge represents "lies" with the power to create a dream of hell. (Draw a picture of a sword, or look for a miniature in a toy store.)

Imagine the word as a magical stone with the power to cast a spell or to break a spell. One side of the stone is black; the other side is white. (Any stone will do, and you can paint it yourself.) The magical stone could also be a gemstone that you wear as a piece of jewelry: a ring, a necklace, or a bracelet. If you select a piece of jewelry, you can wear it every day.

Imagine the word as a musical note or a sound on a musical scale. Some words that you play in your mind will bring you up and lift your spirit; others will bring you down. (Draw a picture of musical notes or find a miniature musical instrument.)

AGREEMENT TO BE IMPECCABLE WITH MY WORD

THIS AGREEMENT is made on _____ (date) for the purpose of increasing my happiness and personal freedom. I am responsible for creating my personal dream of heaven on earth, and it begins with the power of my word.

I choose to be impeccable with my word. I promise to honor myself, to speak with integrity, and to choose my words carefully. I *intend* to use the power of my word in the direction of truth and love. I will pay *attention* to how I use the word. I will take *action* every day to keep my word impeccable. I will *repeat* this action until the habit is firmly established and no longer requires my attention. The symbol of my commitment to this agreement is _____.

Signed: _____

Witness: _____

3

Dreaming

**The function of the human mind is to dream,
but we have learned to dream without awareness.**

*And he realized that everyone was dreaming, but without awareness,
without knowing what they really are.*

—The Smokey Mirror

FROM THE TOLTEC PERSPECTIVE, YOUR ENTIRE LIFE
has been a dream. You are dreaming right now with the
brain awake, and you also dream with the brain asleep.

I know this may be a little difficult to understand,
but if you use your imagination it will be very clear.
Imagine a perfect mirror that reflects what exists outside

of it. Of course, we cannot touch what is inside the mirror because it's only an illusion. What we see inside the mirror is a virtual reality, and we know that it's not real.

It's the same with the human mind. The retina inside the eye is just like a perfect mirror. Everything you see right now is an image created in the retina of your eye. The difference between the mirror and your eye is that behind the eye is the nervous system that analyzes and interprets everything we perceive. The eye, the brain, the mind work so perfectly together that we can swear the image is real. But what we see inside our mind is a virtual reality created by images of light. This reflection of light is the dream.

Light reproduces every image in our eye, it reflects every object, and because it can project an image in such perfect detail, we don't notice that it's light we perceive. The nervous system doesn't notice that we are dreaming. Light creates the human mind with all the different components including the emotions, and it is nothing but a dream.

The dream is ongoing everywhere, not just in humans, but in plants, in rocks, in everything because light puts all the information that comes from Life inside each form of matter. Light is the messenger of Life; it contains all information, all power, all possibilities, and all potential of Life. Light comes from everywhere, and fills everything. Different frequencies of light act as a mold or blueprint for all the different forms of Life. There is only one living being manifesting in billions of forms.

We perceive light that comes from outside us and that light creates the frame of the dream, but we also perceive light reflected in the virtual reality inside our mind. We perceive our own dream, which is also light. When our brain is asleep, the dream has the tendency to change rapidly because there is no frame. Whatever we put our attention onto, whoosh! — our dream changes instantly. When our brain is asleep, everything is possible. We can fly and do all those wonderful things we cannot do when we are awake and the reasoning mind makes our beliefs so rigid.

When the brain is awake, we give form and direction to the whole creation, and we see it as a totality. With that frame we have a notion of time and space; we think it's this day and this hour. The reasoning mind creates the illusion of time and space to justify the dream in our mind. Thinking is dreaming with a language; it is nothing but the effort of the mind to justify the dream. Time and space are an illusion; they are in the virtual reality. All that exists is here and now.

The old shamans would use hallucinogenic plants like peyote to distort the perception of the brain and give you the awareness that you are dreaming. But imagine the brain as a perfect computer. If you pour a cup of coffee inside a computer, you will understand what happens when the human brain is given hallucinogenic drugs. What happens is that it malfunctions. The perception is no longer perfect; the colors mix, the stability changes, and suddenly it is obvious that the mind is running a program; it is dreaming.

Your brain, your eyes, your mind usually think so perfectly that if you see colors mixing, the reasoning mind tries to justify it by saying, "I see God; I am having a spiritual experience." But it's just a malfunction, and it shows us that our brain can create the illusion of a whole reality in this way. I never recommend taking drugs or using power plants because they can hurt the brain, and this is not the point. There is no need to hurt our brain to prove that we are dreaming.

We are living in a world of billions of our kind who don't know they are dreaming. Everyone is also participating in a bigger dream, a society dream. Our dreams overlap and we each dream a part of the entire dream, the *dream of the planet*, which is made by the projection of billions of personal dreams.

Each of us lives in a virtual reality. We have no choice; the mind is programmed to dream, and that can be so beautiful. If you meet someone and you hook his attention, you can start exchanging information, and soon you know a lot about that person's dream. You learn about his friends, what he does, his favorite movies, sports, you name it, depending on what that person projects to you. All those different possibilities are there, and it's a whole distinct reality that is ongoing and as real as any other one.

It can be very exciting when we understand that we are dreaming. Why? Because as soon as we have the awareness that our dream is made of light, then we also know that we can change as fast as light, and our life starts changing right away. We know that we can change our beliefs any time we need to change them because they are no longer rigid. The worries in our life don't look real anymore; we know that it's a dream and it can shift. All the elements of the dream that used to be our knowledge, that used to be trapped inside the belief system, are no longer rigid; they are not the truth anymore, and we know that.

Once we understand that we are dreaming, knowledge doesn't control our faith anymore. Instead, the opposite happens: our faith controls our knowledge; our faith controls our agreements and beliefs. We accept that it's our responsibility to change the dream if we don't like it, and we surrender to being responsible.

Once we understand that we are dreaming, we

know that everybody around us is also dreaming, with or without awareness. Then we realize that the point of view other people use to see the world has nothing to do with us. At this point we no longer even *try* not to take anything personally. We don't take anything personally because we know others are dreaming, and it is only their point of view. Of course, people around us will take things personally. They will use their Book of Law to judge us and to judge everybody else, but now we don't even try to defend ourselves against their Book of Law. We know they are never going to believe what we say anyway unless they change the way they dream.

We don't expect that people will understand us. They are still ruling their lives by their personal Book of Law, and they are still comparing notes with everybody else. We will understand them because we used to be the same way, but they will not understand us.

At this point, we no longer make assumptions. We know it is a fact that others are dreaming, and in their minds whatever they say right now can change the next day or the next instant. The dreamer and the dream are constantly changing and shifting, so how can we make assumptions when we know that everything is changing? We also know that we cannot make the assumption that others are going to be what we want them to be. At this point, we only have two choices: we love them the way they are and respect all the changes in them, or we walk away. We are no longer attached to the outcome, because we have our faith.

Before we are aware that we are dreaming, we make assumptions constantly because knowledge has power over us. Once we have power over knowledge, there's no need to make assumptions. Knowledge becomes a tool that we use to communicate. We can ask and we can understand; we can express ourselves, and we can listen to other people express their own dream.

At this point, our whole life becomes magic. Miracles happen, and they happen all the time. There is only one thing we can use to guide our actions, reactions, and our interactions with all those dreamers who don't have awareness, and that is our integrity. Our integrity is who we really are, the totality of our own self.

Those who are ruling their lives by the Book of Law, have the *illusion* of integrity, but they don't really have it. Every time they reject themselves, it's a lack of integrity. Every time they believe they are not perfect, it's a lack of integrity. Every time they suffer, every time they get jealous or angry or envious, every time they create a drama, they are going against themselves, and it's a lack of integrity.

We recover our integrity when we are impeccable with our word. We lost our integrity the first time we broke our word, the first time we went against our own self. Self-betrayal is what breaks our integrity. From that point on, all our loyalty was to the Book of Law. Whatever goes against the Book of Law looks like it goes against our integrity, but that is not exactly true because we are using that book against our own self. We are using it for self-rejection, for all those agreements that lead us into emotional drama.

Once we are aware that we are dreaming, the Book of Law is broken, we recover our integrity, and we can feel it. Before the Book of Law is broken, we are not following our integrity; we are following the rules of the book. Concepts like guilt, blame, right, wrong, loyalty, and patriotism for the country, all affect us very deeply because we believe in them. And this makes us very easy prey for manipulation by the dream of the planet. Even concepts like what is beautiful or ugly are agreements that control society and later control the individual mind. We give our power to these agreements, we become a slave to them; then other people use those values to manipulate us. Once the Book of Law is broken, these values are no longer a tool of manipulation between humans.

When you recover your integrity, you can no longer go to someone and ask him for his approval, because you are asking for the approval of his Book of Law. The only answer he can give you is according to his Book of Law, which isn't any good to you. You need to trust yourself. You cannot go to someone and say,

"Is what I'm doing right? Is what I'm doing wrong?" No. You are alone, and thank God you are alone because it means you are free to be yourself again, and your integrity will not allow you to go against yourself. You will know that you have recovered your integrity when you feel good, when you feel happy. Every time you don't feel good it's the result of a self-judgment, and that judgment is using the Book of Law to find you guilty. Now you are ashamed of yourself, and that's why you don't feel good.

The Four Agreements help us to align with our integrity. The first agreement, *impeccability of the word,* is completely aligned with our integrity. The second and third agreements, *don't take anything personally,* and *don't make assumptions,* give us immunity to the Book of Law and to everybody else around us. With that immunity, we can be assured that the outside dream will not choose our beliefs for us again. And the fourth agreement, *always do your best,* is the engine that moves us forward; it is the action.

The dream is alive, and it can change as fast as light, as fast as Life. When our awareness is there — in the light instead of the fog, in our faith instead of our knowledge — we recover our faith, our will, and our power. And we find that we have the power to make choices, to take risks, to project, to perceive, to interact, and to master the dream. We can become a dream artist and create the most beautiful masterpiece of art with the dream of our life.

To create a masterpiece instead of a nightmare, instead of emotional dramas, can be very exciting. But if we are not aware that it's a dream, there is no way to change the dream. Most people are born, grow old, and die, and never notice that all of life is a dream, so they become trapped in their own nightmare. When we live without this awareness, something inside us is telling us all the time, *it is a dream, this can't be real.* But we are not sure that it is a dream; it could be *real.*

The reasoning mind is in the virtual reality, and it has no awareness that it's in the virtual reality, so it tries to justify, explain, and make sense of everything. The reasoning mind always wants answers. Even if the answers are wrong, those answers make us feel safe. That is why humans make all those assumptions, create all those theories, and all that knowledge that is completely untrue. Look at the knowledge of European society five or six hundred years ago, and you see a lot of books explaining the world of the angels, the world of the demons, life after death, going to heaven, and going to hell.

That mythology is beautiful, that art is beautiful, but it's not truth. It is nothing but mythology; it is candy for the reasoning mind and it's far from the truth, but it provided a structure that made those humans feel safe. Yet that knowledge was also used to judge people, condemn people, and even to kill them. How many people were killed during the Inquisition? How many people were burned to death because they were *believed* to be witches or because they *didn't believe* that the earth was the center of the universe?

Humanity has progressed a lot. Just by having the awareness that the whole society is dreaming, you can see all the possibilities; you can see that we are going in the right direction. But of course, in order to change the whole society, we first have to change ourselves.

PRACTICE IDEA FOR MASTERING AWARENESS
YOUR AUTHENTIC SELF

Once he knew what he really was, he looked around at other humans and the rest of nature, and he was amazed at what he saw.

Your integrity is who you really are, what you really are, the totality of your authentic self. Spend a few moments every day to get in touch with the memory of what you are. Allow yourself to imagine the possibility that you are made by a certain frequency of Light. Light is the messenger of God; it contains all information, all possibilities, and all power. Imagine that you are made of Light, of Spirit. There is nothing you need to do. There is nothing you need to be except what you really are. Remember what you are, and the dream of your Life will have no limits.

PART TWO

Mastering Transformation

4

The Second Attention

Using your will and attention for the second time.

Now it's up to you to choose what to believe and what not to believe. You can choose to believe in anything, and that includes believing in yourself.

THE FIRST TIME OUR ATTENTION IS USED, WE ARE innocent. As children we are programmed to dream the way the outside dreams; we have no choice. Someone either hooks our attention to teach us, or we focus our attention to learn.

The attention is that part of our mind that can discriminate and concentrate on whatever we want to perceive. Where we put our attention, is what we experience — our personal dream.

The dream you are living right now is the result of the humans around you hooking your attention and feeding you all of their beliefs. If someone hooks your attention, you think it's your decision and will to do it, but that decision is nothing but a habit; it's only a program. It is just as if the outside pushes a button and everything inside you knows what to do; it knows what reaction to have.

We say that humans have free will, but this is hardly true. Our will is controlled by the dream of the planet; our attention is hooked by the outside dream, and we follow the will of the outside. In the program mode, we push a button and start walking; we push another button and we walk to the right, we walk to the left, or we stop. Just by action–reaction we automatically have the response — physical, emotional, all kinds of responses that are already in the program.

If we had free will, would we choose to be angry, or sad, or envious? It's obvious to me that it's not our choice. Of course, we can lie to ourselves and say, "I have free will; I can make a choice." But every time we suffer, that proves we don't have the power to make a choice. If we had free will, we would never choose to be victimized because when we are victimized, we are angry, we have all that fear. If we had free will, we would never choose anything that would hurt us, ever. And we would certainly never choose to hurt the people that we love.

What the Toltec call *the second attention* is about learning to use our attention for the second time to begin the transformation of our dream. In the dream of the second attention, we control our attention from the inside, escape the dream of the planet, and create a brand new dream: our personal dream of heaven on earth.

In the dream of the second attention, we live in the same world, but with a difference. The difference is that now we are no longer innocent; we can choose to believe whatever we want to believe. Using our awareness, we can focus our attention in our everyday life to reprogram ourselves in our own way.

In the dream of the second attention, we find out that we are responsible for our choices. What we agree to believe is our own choice, not the choice of the images we think we are, not the choice from our ego who pretends to know everything, but a choice from our own integrity. In the new dream, we only put our faith in agreements that support Life, which add to our joy, to our happiness, to our freedom. We break the agreements based on lies, and we make new agreements based on truth. The whole meaning and perception of our dream changes because our agreements have changed. In the dream of the second attention, we find that everything is possible. But to dream this way, we first need to control our attention from the inside.

Let's say someone calls my name, "Miguel." That hooks my attention and I turn and say, "What do you want?" That person says what she wants, and if I'm interested, if I care about it, I'm there. But I make the choice whether I care about it or not. The moment I'm not interested, I just unhook and say, "Forget it," and my attention goes in other directions.

That's the reason some people think I have a bad memory. It's not because I'm getting old or something else going on with my brain. What happens is that people hook my attention, and I put my attention on what they tell me. If whatever they say is not aligning with my dream, with my beliefs, then I see their dream and share a conversation, but their dream is not my business, and I let it go. I unhook my attention and I am living in the moment. I'm not living in the past; I'm not carrying those thought forms any longer. A few minutes later, I just forget what the conversation was about because there is no place in my dream for all the drama humans create. If someone asks me what that person said, I don't remember. It was long ago even though it was just that morning.

But let's say I find something very interesting. My attention is hooked, and I'm there in every moment because that is my choice. Then, yes, the outside can hook my attention, but what hooks my attention and keeps my attention — that's another story. I will not give my attention just because the outside requires my attention. It's not necessary for me to be interested in what someone else is doing. I will not go against myself by keeping my attention where I don't want it to be. Whatever I do, I'm going to be there in a way that is interesting to me, in a way that I can do my best because I want to, not because I have to; in a way that fulfills me more, and is better for other people too.

Of course, this doesn't mean the outside dream has given up; the outside dream is programmed to dream the dream of hell. The outside dream still has all that knowledge, all those opinions, and it will try to put those seeds in our mind and hook us again from the outside. One of the easiest ways is through gossip. The agreement humans have with one another is to interact using the transference of emotional poison. How do we transfer emotional poison from one person to another? By hooking the attention of the other person.

If we have a lot of anger, for example, we know the way to feel better is to release the anger. But we have learned that to release the anger, we need to hook someone's attention. By hooking someone's attention and expressing and venting the anger, we feel better, but now the other person has that poison. Now the other person feels the anger, or the jealousy, or whatever emotional poison was sent.

By hooking the attention, almost any kind of energy can be transferred from one mind to another mind, including love. Humans are always searching for someone whose attention they can hook and manipulate because we were all domesticated to compete for the control of one another's attention. That's why you see the war of control in human relationships. It's a war between the inside dream and the outside dream — a war between humans and the dream of the planet over who will control the attention.

The outside dream controls the personal dream by hooking the attention of whoever doesn't have free will. It can and will strike hard even at those who do have free will. In any moment we can be hooked by the outside dream. If this happens, the key is to unhook ourselves as fast as we can and keep the awareness.

For example: Imagine that I said to you, "You're a liar." If you believe it, your attention gets hooked, and it's a sign that you really believe what you're hearing. Just because I said that, I put your attention in a wound that you have. If you control your attention from the inside, you see the wound, and you can use your attention to shift your belief. In this moment, you can choose to no longer believe you are a liar; your attention controls the belief, and you are healed. An hour later, if I come to you and say, "You're a liar," you have no reaction anymore, because it is no longer your belief. But if you get hurt, it's because you still have that wound; it's because you believe me.

Without free will, your beliefs control your attention. If you control your attention from the inside, you decide when your attention is hooked by the outside and you recover free will. Once you recover free will, your attention controls your beliefs.

Everybody around you is a mirror that is going to reflect your wounds. Whoever comes and lets you know where your wounds are is doing you a big favor. That person is putting your attention on the place where you have a wound, but perhaps you didn't know you had one. And if you have free will and your attention controls your beliefs, just by putting your awareness on the wound, you can shift it. You can say, "Oh, thank you for being a mirror and letting me see my wounds."

Whoever crosses you becomes the best mirror, the best way for you to measure your own evolution. You don't know how well you are doing before you have the challenge. When it's just yourself, it's hard to see. You can think you are doing so well, and you can go to an ashram and stay there for five years. Maybe you meditate and spend five years not eating meat, not having sex, and doing other things to transform your life. You feel very good about yourself, but then someone comes and crosses you, and boom! You need another five years in that ashram.

In a situation like that, if you don't react, you see your own evolution. You can see that the way you used to be is no longer true. You observe it and think, "Wow, I'm doing well. I'm in a situation where you are going against me, and look at me, I'm happy. I even love you."

We don't need to escape from life; we don't need to deny our own nature. What we need is complete awareness and self-acceptance. We need to learn to make our own choices and finally control our will from the inside. With that, if someone crosses us, we just shift our attention and recover our free will. That is what makes us a dream master. Where we choose to put our attention is what creates the miracle.

PRACTICE IDEA FOR MASTERING TRANSFORMATION
THE DREAM OF THE SECOND ATTENTION

One way to change your beliefs is to focus your attention on all those agreements and beliefs, and change the agreements with yourself. In doing this, you are using your attention for the second time, thus creating the dream of the second attention or the new dream.

Are you aware of how you use your attention? Imagine what your new dream will look like when you create it the way that *you* choose. What does your *new* dream say about how you choose to treat yourself? What does it say about how you choose to relate to other people, to other forms of Life, to God? In the dream of the second attention, you have the right to be happy, the right to express your creativity, the right to have abundance, the right to be who you really are.

The Book of Law practice ideas at the end of Chapter One focused on identifying the self-limiting, fear-based beliefs that limit your personal freedom and rob you of your happiness. By now, you have taken an inventory of many of these beliefs and agreements, and through this process you have begun the transformation. Now you are going to rewrite your Book of Law by creating a new set of agreements based on love and truth instead of fear and lies.

Use a brand new journal to record the beliefs and agreements you will choose in the new dream of your life. Here are some title ideas for your journal:

The Dream of the Second Attention
The Art of Dreaming
My New Dream of Life
My New Book of Law

Just as you did before, create chapter headings for at least four important areas of your life:

Personal Agreements: Your Body and Your Self
Social Agreements: Family and Friends
Spiritual Agreements: Life and God
Financial Agreements: Work and Career

You may want to use the same headings, words, and descriptions that you chose for your first Book of Law. After you enter the chapter headings in your journal, consider what you choose to believe about each of these areas of your life.

Go back and review all the self-limiting, fear-based beliefs you identified earlier, and the new agreements you wrote to replace each one of these beliefs. Then consider how you can transform your habits and routines by controlling your attention from the inside.

You have to know which agreements you want to change before you can change them.

To change an agreement, focus your attention on the agreement you want to change. Only you know which agreements are not working for you.

Begin by asking yourself the following questions:

What areas of my life present a challenge for me at the moment?

What specific problem do I want to resolve?

What unpleasant emotions am I feeling?

What actions or choices are leading me to these unpleasant feelings?

What agreements have I made that support these actions?

What actions can I take to change the reaction?

What agreements would support these actions?

Look at your answers to the above questions. Even if an action appears to go against someone else, if it makes you feel guilty, ashamed, or unhappy, it goes against you too. Here is an example:

The area of my life that is most challenging for me at the moment is being a parent.

The specific problem I want to resolve is to be a better parent to my children.

The unpleasant emotion I am feeling is guilt.

The actions I am taking that lead me to this feeling are:

1. I am yelling at my children when they don't listen to me.

2. I spend most of my time taking care of chores, and I don't spend quality time with my children.

The agreements I have made that support these actions are:

1. I have agreed that it's okay to yell at my children when they don't listen to me.

2. I have agreed that it's okay to let other things pull my attention and keep me from spending quality time with my children.

The actions I can take that would change the reaction are:

1. I can stop yelling at my children.

2. I can spend more time with my children.

The agreements that support these actions are:

1. I don't agree that it's okay to yell at my children. I choose to speak to my children in a firm but loving tone, even when I am upset with them.

2. I don't agree that it's okay to let other things take my attention away from my children. I choose to spend quality time with my children every day.

Remember, you achieve the Mastery of Transformation by changing the agreements that make you suffer, and reprogramming your own mind, in your own way. Another way to do this is to adopt alternative agreements such as the Four Agreements, and make them your personal code of conduct. Using the above example, go through each of the Four Agreements and ask yourself what actions you would take as a parent if you were living your life by these principles.

We can declare a war against the Parasite, a war against the Judge and the Victim, a war for our independence, a war for the right to use our own mind and our own brain.

Declare a war against the Parasite

The decision to adopt the Four Agreements is a declaration of war to regain your freedom from the Parasite, which is the Judge, the Victim, and the Book of Law. Write the following statement out three times, and place each copy of the declaration where it will remind you of your commitment to personal freedom:

"I declare a war against my Parasite for the freedom to use my own mind and body, for the freedom to become the architect of my own life, to design the life of my dreams, and to create a masterpiece of art."

The old agreements that rule our dream of life are the result of repeating them over and over again. To adopt the Four Agreements, you need to put repetition in action. Repetition makes the master.

TOOLS FOR TRANSFORMATION

Take a moment to consider how you memorize a phone number. The number doesn't get stored in your memory until you agree to store it. Once you agree, you use your will and your attention to commit the number to memory. Keep this process in mind as you create the dream of the second attention. Use the tools of intention, attention, action, and repetition:

Intention: Set your intention; make a commitment to change the agreement. This paves the way for action.

Attention: Learn to control your attention from the inside. Be aware that so many things in the outside dream will compete for your attention.

Action: Take action. Without action, there will be no change, no growth, no reward.

Repetition: Practice and practice the action until the new agreement is firmly established and programmed in your memory. Repetition makes the master.

For example:

Intention: I intend to master the Four Agreements.

Attention: I will pay attention to my thoughts, feelings, and actions each day.

Action: I will take the following actions every day to ensure that I keep my new agreements: . . .

Repetition: I will repeat these actions for at least four weeks.

Just like hell, heaven is a place that exists within our mind. It is a place of joy, a place where we are happy, where we are free to love and to be who we really are. We can reach heaven while we are alive; we don't have to wait until we die.

HEAVEN ON EARTH

What is your idea of heaven on earth? Have you ever taken the time to consider this? Describe your dream in full detail.

Are you aware of what gives you the greatest joy?

I feel the greatest joy whenever I . . .

Are you aware of what inspires you, or what makes your spirit soar?

I am most inspired whenever I . . .

The last judgment

Spend the next twenty minutes using your imagination to dream a new dream.

Imagine how your life would be if today was the day of your last judgment; if after today, you no longer judged yourself, and you no longer judged other people.

Imagine if the voice of knowledge in your head no longer talked to you; if that voice in your head left you alone, and you only followed your heart.

Imagine if the voice of knowledge was silent because you don't need to think about what you know; you don't need to learn to be what you are.

Imagine if you could express what you are with joy instead of judgment.

What does it *feel* like? Capture the feeling and remember the feeling. This is the beginning of a new dream.

5

Action–Reaction

Using the Four Agreements to change your actions–reactions.

Dream masters create a masterpiece of life; they control the dream by making choices. Everything has consequences, and a dream master is aware of the consequences.

EVERY ACTION HAS A REACTION, AND FOR ALL OF our life we repeat our actions and suffer the same reactions. Perhaps we cannot see the action or the choices when we make them, but we are always going to see the reaction, the result of what we do. Many times there are things in our lives that we don't like, that we want to change, but we make the same mistakes, the same choices, expecting that the result will be different. Well, it will not be different.

The only way to change your life is to change the choices, to change the actions. If there is something in your life that you don't like, first you have to be aware that it is the result of something that you do. It's the result of a choice that you made. Then if you take one step back and focus your attention on what is happening just before that result, you will find what you did that isn't working, what you did that caused the result you don't want.

Once you find out what action you took, the next step is to forgive the reaction and change the choice, change the action, and see what the reaction is. If you don't like the result again, you change it again and again until you have the result you want.

Perhaps you cannot control what is going to happen around you, but you can certainly control your own reaction. Your reaction is the clue to having a wonderful life. Why? Because what makes you happy or unhappy is not what is happening around you, but how you choose to react to it. If you can learn to change your own reactions, then you can change your habits and routines, change the program, and change your life.

Imagine that ten years ago you made a big mistake in the eyes of everybody. Everybody judged you harshly, and you judged yourself harshly also. But just because you made a mistake, does that mean you should suffer for the rest of your life? This is not fair. Your reaction is that you live with shame, with guilt, and low self-esteem; your reaction is that you feel you are worthless and you want to end your life, and perhaps you don't even know why.

Well, take a step back, and you will find out why. It's because you are still taking the same action, and that leads to the same reaction. You think you are still suffering for what happened ten years ago, but that is not true. The truth is that you are suffering for what happened a minute ago, or thirty seconds ago. The *excuse* for your suffering is "I made a terrible mistake ten years ago." The *truth* is that you judged yourself thirty seconds ago.

If you find that you are living your life in shame or guilt right now, look one step before you felt guilt, and you will see that you judged yourself. What was the action–reaction? The *action* was self-judgment; the *action* was self-rejection. The *reaction* is that you find yourself guilty, and you believe it. Your faith is there and your faith says, "I need to be punished." *Thy will be done;* you are going to be punished.

Now let's see how the Four Agreements can help you break the old agreement to judge and punish yourself, and create a new agreement to forgive yourself.

Thirty seconds ago when you judged yourself, you were not impeccable with your word. When you judged yourself, you used your word against yourself.

Thirty seconds ago, you took it personally — something that happened ten years ago! It is a ghost in your mind, it is no longer true, but you took it personally.

Thirty seconds ago, you made a big assumption that everybody remembers what you did ten years ago, and that everybody is still condemning you.

Thirty seconds ago, you didn't do your best, because the action you took made you feel miserable.

Now you know you feel miserable because thirty seconds ago you judged yourself. If you don't want to feel miserable, you have to change the action that caused the reaction. First, you have to be impeccable with your word. You *really* make a commitment to be impeccable. Whenever you have the memory of what happened ten years ago, instead of judging yourself, you can change the action and say, "I forgive myself." Then the reaction will also change. Isn't that logical? It is just common sense. "I forgive myself." Now you are impeccable with your word.

Second, you will not take anything personally. That means even if you made a mistake, and other people react and judge, it's nothing personal. You know that they live in their own dream.

Third, you don't make assumptions about what other people think of you. There is no way you will ever know what is in their head or how they dream.

Finally, you are going to do your best. But there is only one way to do your best, and that is doing it. Not saying "I will do it," or "I will try." It's the action that will make the difference.

The action is first to use your awareness, to be aware that if you are unhappy, it is because of an action you took. Second, to use your attention to focus on the action–reaction and identify what action you took. Look one step before you began to feel unhappy, and you will see what the action is. Third, to shift your attention to the Four Agreements and apply them to every action–reaction. Using this process, every action–reaction of your life can be shifted like this: awareness, attention, action–reaction. The result is very powerful.

My suggestion is to keep focusing your attention through your integrity, and make choices that don't go against yourself. By focusing your attention and following your integrity, you can measure your choices by your action–reaction. This choice comes from love; that choice comes from fear. This choice makes me happy; that choice makes me suffer.

The difficult part is to be aware. Everything we learn from the outside dream goes against awareness; we practice every agreement we create, and our agreements go against our awareness. But we can also practice awareness until we recover awareness. To recover our awareness, we have to break our agreements with knowledge, and reaffirm our commitment to honor the Four Agreements.

The Four Agreements go against the majority of the agreements in our Book of Law and help us to detach the information from the Parasite. They will help break the code of the program in our mind, but they need to be practiced, and the only way to do that is by focusing our attention.

To change our agreements, we first have to know which agreements we want to change. Then we have to have enough personal power to change our agreements because it is not our reasoning mind that can change them. The way to do it is to focus our attention on the agreement we want to change, and use the power of our word, our intent, to make a new agreement that we will not believe the old agreement. If we don't believe something, we agree that it's not true, and we unlearn that agreement.

For every agreement we break, we need to replace it with a new agreement. If there is an agreement that makes us suffer, and we break it but don't replace it with another agreement that will make us happy, the old agreement will come back. If we withdraw our faith in the old agreement, and invest it in the new agreement, then the old agreement is gone forever and now we believe the new agreement.

Practicing the new agreements in our lives is how our best becomes better. Once we learn a new agreement, we don't need to focus our attention on it any longer; it becomes automatic, and our response is always the same. All those old agreements we have that rule our dream of life are the result of repeating them over and over again.

Let's look at an emotional routine like getting angry. Anger is fear with a mask, and at a certain point in your interaction with someone, you were afraid and got angry. Your anger pushed that person away, he left you alone, and you found that getting angry worked. The same situation happened again and again, and anger became a routine. It became an agreement with yourself that you need anger to feel safe. Later you discover that anger pushes people away even when you don't want it to, and you are alone. People don't like you because of your anger, but by then you forget why you were angry in the first place. You don't know why anger has become a normal reaction for you or why every time you are afraid you get angry.

The routine has been repeated thousands of times and it becomes a normal reaction for you; you are conditioned to behave that way. That is the challenge: to be aware, to change the routine, to change the action. Again, the first step is always to be aware and to practice awareness until you master awareness. Without awareness, there is no way for you to change your choices or change your actions. With awareness, you focus your attention, put repetition in action, and change your agreements and routines.

The repeated action of using the Four Agreements will break many of the agreements that make life so difficult and unpleasant. It takes a lot of time and courage because it's easier just to take things personally, make assumptions, and react the way you react all the time. But that leads you into emotional pain, and your reaction is to send the poison back to other people and increase the drama. When you can stop the drama at the very beginning, you solve the problem right away, and there is nothing else to do after that.

In the beginning, create something to remind you to keep your attention on this process and to practice it again and again until you master it. Once you start, you will see the results, and it gets easier and easier. Eventually there will come a time when it becomes automatic. Once it becomes a habit, the transformation of your life starts happening fast, and you start changing as fast as life changes. You see the changes and your self-respect increases, your enthusiasm rises, and self-acceptance returns to your life.

PRACTICE IDEA FOR MASTERING TRANSFORMATION
AWARENESS, ATTENTION, ACTION–REACTION

You need a very strong will in order to adopt the Four Agreements, but if you can begin to live your life with these agreements, the transformation in your life will be amazing. You will see the drama of hell disappear right before your very eyes.

DIRECT YOUR OWN DRAMA

Think of a recent event in your life that caused a lot of emotional pain. Now try to imagine this event from a "distant" perspective; that is, try to detach yourself emotionally from the actions–reactions that are part of this event.

Once you create some emotional distance between you and the event, imagine yourself as the director of a dramatic play in which the same scene is unfolding upon a stage. As you view the stage from the balcony of the theater, you can clearly observe the part each character has in the play. You also have the power to direct their actions– reactions in any way you choose.

Make a list of the cast of characters involved in this event. Who took the action that first triggered the drama? What was the reaction?

Here are some additional questions to consider:

Who had the leading role in the play?

What was your role in this drama?

What actions did you take?

What were the reactions of the other people involved in the play?

How did you react to their actions?

What other actions did you take?

What were the results?

Now consider the above information from the perspective of applying the Four Agreements:

Were you impeccable with your word?

Did you take anything personally?

Did you make assumptions?

Did you do your best?

Instant replay: what might have happened if . . .

> You had been impeccable with your word?
>
> You had not taken things personally?
>
> You had not made assumptions?
>
> You had done your best?

What might have happened if all the other characters in the drama . . .

> Had been impeccable with their word?
>
> Had not taken things personally?
>
> Had not made assumptions?
>
> Had done their best?

Use your imagination to envision this event so that: (1) you can practice mastering awareness of your part in the drama, and (2) you can practice mastering transformation of the dream by using the Four Agreements to create a more satisfying outcome.

Can you imagine yourself avoiding this kind of drama in the future? If not, why not?

Think of another emotionally painful experience and repeat the steps above. Practice transforming these events in your imagination with the Four Agreements as your guiding principles.

The next time anything threatens to sabotage your happiness, you will be prepared to use the Four Agreements to transform your actions–reactions and experience a whole new dream. Keep a record of each dramatic event in your journal so you can track your progress.

6

Attach–Detach

Surrendering to the angel of death.

The Parasite wants us to carry the past with us, and that makes it so heavy to be alive. When we try to live in the past, how can we enjoy the present?

EVERYTHING THAT EXISTS IS IN AN ETERNAL transformation. Everything in nature, all of creation, is changing. Creation is happening in the moment. It has no beginning, it has no end; it is ongoing. Energy is always transforming because it is alive.

Life is the force that makes the transformation of energy possible. The force of Life that opens a flower is the same force that makes us grow older. Look at your physical body, and just imagine how you used to look when you were five years old compared with now. It still is you, but the body is completely different. It has changed.

The dream of the planet is also changing, but more slowly than the personal dream. Even matter, the frame of the dream, is always changing. Some things change so slowly that we don't notice them changing, but in one year we notice the change, or in ten years we notice the change. The buildings we live in are changing, although very slowly. The trees and the mountains — all of nature is changing because Life is passing through everything and everything is reacting to Life.

Our personal dream, the whole interaction between the dream and the dreamer, is constantly shifting and changing. But in the virtual reality in our mind, we try to stop things from changing. Humans get attached to the dream; we resist the transformation of Life. And this attachment, this resistance, creates emotional pain.

By resisting the transformation of Life, humans create the illusion of death; we suffer from every "loss" again and again. Humans have a powerful memory and we witness our own dream. In our memory we attach to what is past, we try to bring it back to life, and in the virtual reality we succeed.

We create a whole movie in our mind that we can repeat as often as we want to. If we close our eyes and use our imagination, we can see the movie again and again in the same way, from our point of view, of course, with our own interpretation that is only true for us. We modify our memories and distort the images; what we remember is not the way things really happened, but the movie keeps playing in our mind.

Life is what is happening; death is what is not happening. A moment after something happens, it is already dead. Whatever happened to us as a child, in school, with friends, in love relationships — whatever was true thirty years ago — is no longer true. Our whole personal history is dead, but we become so attached that we bring back the ghost in our mind.

We carry the memory of our whole life knowing that it is dead, that it is no longer true, and yet it affects our everyday life. It is true that the memory happened, but it's also true that it is not happening anymore. It is gone; it isn't real. If it was real, it's no longer real.

In our dream, we keep death alive because we attach to what is dead, but death doesn't really exist. Only Life, only creation, exists. The past is just an illusion. The angel of death teaches us to live in the present moment, which is the only moment we truly have. When we resist transformation and want to live in the past, we are still living in the present moment, but we are focused in a past dream. By focusing our attention in a past dream, our attention is not in the present, and we are not fully alive.

Toltec mythology tells us that the angel of death is always beside us, ready to take everything away from us. Everything belongs to the angel of death. Nothing is ours to keep, including our physical body. Knowing this, we surrender to the angel of death and accept the transformation of Life.

The angel of death takes everything away from us little by little. But for everything the angel of death takes away, Life gives us something new. If we become so attached to what the angel of death is taking away, then we cannot receive the gifts of Life.

What the Toltec call "surrendering to the angel of death" can also be called "detachment." Detachment doesn't mean that we stop loving someone or something; it only means we accept that there is nothing we can do to stop the transformation of Life. Detachment is so powerful because when we learn to detach, we respect the forces of nature, which means we also respect the changes in our own life.

By nature we are born with the capacity to adapt to transformation, to adapt to constant change. When we are little children, we always live in the present moment; we don't worry about the future, and we don't care about the past. Instinctively we let go of what is past, and we accept every gift that life brings. If we are playing with a toy and we get bored, we let it go; we leave it in the grass and we no longer care about that toy until it hooks our attention again. If we lose the toy and it's no longer there, we turn our attention to another toy. Little children accept the transformation of life, just as all animals do. Domestication teaches us to try to live in the past, and to project into the future. After domestication, humans hardly ever live in the present moment.

One way to practice surrendering to the angel of death is by practicing what I call "attach–detach." Perhaps by calling it "attach–detach" you can see that it is something you can practice in your daily life. When something comes to you, you attach and enjoy it as intensely as you can. As soon as the moment passes, you detach and let it go. You don't need to pay attention to what is gone, to what is already dead. When your attention is in the present, you aren't carrying the burdens of the past.

If you can master attachment and detachment, you will keep your attention in the present moment. With awareness and practice, you are always going to enjoy your life because whatever is before you, you are going to give 100 percent of your attention. You are going to take all the action necessary to enjoy your life, and detach from whatever is gone.

For example: I may love a woman very deeply, but as soon as I want to own her, I am attached, and I don't want to let her go. No matter what I do, she is free, and every time she walks away from me, if I am attached, it's going to hurt. If I am detached, I respect her freedom. She can do whatever she wants to do, and it doesn't hurt me at all.

By being detached, I respect my own freedom as well. When you are around me, I enjoy your beauty and your presence, and I attach to you. But when I walk out of the door and I do not see you, then I detach because if I don't detach, it's going to hurt. The key is to find an equilibrium between attachment and detachment. Attachment helps you to live your life intensely in the present moment. With attachment you can increase your desire to accomplish whatever you want to accomplish, and with detachment you don't have to suffer what you didn't accomplish. You simply let go.

The practice of attach—detach can be used with business, with homes, with cars, with pets, with everything. But it's even more important with knowledge. Humans become very attached to knowledge. We are so attached to what we believe that we don't want to let go of our beliefs even if these beliefs are not true at all. Even if our beliefs make us suffer and create a big drama in our life, they also make us feel safe because it's a behavior that we know so well.

For all of our life we have carried a corpse with us. That corpse is what we believe we are; it is the human form and all those distorted images we identify with. It is dead and heavy and it rules our life, but we don't want to let it go. We know our limitations, we know how to suffer, we know how to react with jealousy, with anger, and all that emotional drama makes us feel secure. As we said before, letting go of what we know, of what we believe, always creates a little fear and anxiety because we are going into unknown territory.

We don't have to attach to our beliefs. If we are not attached to our beliefs and a better concept comes to us, we can let go of the old concept, adopt the new concept, and improve our life much faster. We can let go of the distorted images we identify with. We can detach from the agreements and beliefs that limit the expression of our creativity and our love. This frees our energy to create a new dream. And what we create is a masterpiece of art: our own life.

PRACTICE IDEA FOR MASTERING TRANSFORMATION
ATTACH–DETACH

Yes, you are going to have memories of the parasite — of the Judge, the Victim, and what you used to believe — but the Parasite will be dead.

Make a list of everything that you feel a strong attachment to, including people, things, events, feelings, agreements, and beliefs. How much energy do you spend trying to resist change or transformation? If you have ever tried to paddle a boat upstream, you know how much energy is wasted by going against the currents of the stream. To resist transformation is to spend energy fighting *against* the current instead of flowing *with* it. Consider the following questions about the items on your list of attachments:

How much emotional and physical energy is required each day to maintain your attachments?

If you could assign a price up to $1000 for each attachment, what does each one cost you?

Is this really how you want to spend your energy?

What else could you do with the energy you invest in your attachments?

Are you ready to practice attach–detach with any of the items on your list of attachments? Start with an object you own that you adore and feel an attachment to. On a scale of one to ten, with number one being total attachment and number ten being total detachment, how would you rate your attachment to this object?

On the attach–detach scale, I would rate this object . . .

I . . . 2 . . . 3 . . . 4 . . . 5 . . . 6 . . . 7 . . . 8 . . . 9 . . . I0

If you selected number five, perhaps you experience a good equilibrium between attachment and detachment. You really enjoy this object and "attach" when it hooks your attention, but if it were damaged or taken away, you could "detach" without suffering through weeks or years of regret. If the number you selected falls below the number five, you may want to practice a little detachment. Begin by listing the reasons you believe you are attached to the object.

Here are some examples:

It was a gift from someone who is special to me.
It is one of a kind; there is none other like it in the world.
It cost a lot of money.
It is very old and irreplaceable (an antique or collectible).

Now consider how much energy you spend each month on your attachment to this object. How much of your attention and physical energy is spent . . .

Protecting this object from other people?
Keeping this object in perfect condition?
Paying for maintenance or protection of this object?
Worrying about this object for whatever reason?

Look at your answers to the above list. Is your attachment based on fear? For example: fear that this object can never be replaced if it's lost; fear that you will lose the good feelings you associate or "attach" to this object; fear that you won't ever have the money to buy another object like this; fear that if you do let go of your attachment, something terrible might happen; fear that you have to control Life because you cannot trust Life.

Try to remember a time in your life when something you were attached to was lost or taken away from you. What did Life give to you in return for what was lost? What personal qualities, such as compassion for others, did you develop as a result of this experience?

DETACHING FROM YOUR BELIEFS

Go back to your Book of Law and look at the list of fear-based agreements you want to change. Are you attached to any of these beliefs and agreements? If so, what purpose do these agreements serve? It is up to you to choose the kind of knowledge you attach to. Set your intention to practice detaching from the knowledge that goes against you or anyone else. Just imagine all of the energy and personal power you will reclaim!

ZOOM IN, ZOOM OUT

Think of a problem in your life that has caused you to worry or suffer. Imagine that you can view your life through the lens of a magical camera. When you zoom in, you see and feel every detail and facet of your life; anything that touches your life comes into focus within the frame of the viewfinder.

Imagine that you can also zoom out whenever you choose in order to see the larger picture of your life. In the zoom-out mode, your focus is no longer on all the details. The first thing you see is the house you live in from hundreds of feet above the ground. In the zoom-out mode, you observe ever-widening panoramic views of first the city where you live, then the country, then the continent, until suddenly you are staring at the earth from outer space.

Pause for a moment to consider your life from this perspective. Your life and all your troubles are a tiny speck on the face of the earth. All your dreams, all your desires, all your hopes and fears are there in that speck on earth. You are there in the midst of billions of people just like you who share similar emotions and dreams. Stay in the zoom-out mode, and continue on your journey into outer space until you can see all the planets in our solar system.

Keep going farther and farther until the entire Milky Way is visible from light-years away.

Who are you? What are you? Where is your place in this vast universe? Why do humans suffer over so many small things in life when there is a universe of beauty and wonder to behold? When we consider the span of eternity, and the entire history of humanity, our life is over in a mere fraction of time. How will we choose to spend it? What will we invest our energy in?

Keep zooming out until you detach completely from your problem and can see that it is insignificant in the greater scheme of Life. Remind yourself that every problem carries the seeds of opportunity to learn, to love, to grow in awareness, and simply to be happy to be alive.

When we attach to an object, to our beliefs, to a person we love, it is just as if we are stuck in the zoom-in mode, and all we can see is the smallest part of Life. We can only see our own life, our own problems; all our worries and attachments come into focus and fill the entire frame of our dream. As we zoom out, our problems represent a smaller and smaller percentage of our entire universe, and we find that they really don't require much of our attention at all.

The next time you find yourself focusing incessantly on a problem, imagine zooming out with your magical camera. Detach from all the details, and put your attention on the wider picture of your life. Remember that nothing in life is truly serious. Imagine that you can enjoy every person, every material possession, every event in your life as a magical experience that continues to unfold.

Zoom out and keep going farther and farther into space until the cord that keeps you attached to your fears finally snaps. As soon as you detach from the fear, you detach from the problem, you detach from the outcome, and you are free. You are floating effortlessly in the stream of Life. When you have no fear, you have no resistance. And when you have no resistance, the solution to your problem is there in the Light, and it comes to you. The solution to every problem of humanity is in the Light.

You are alive, you are free, and you are powerful. You are not a victim of your beliefs, your desires, your society, or your circumstance. You are an active participant in the art of dreaming.

PART THREE

Living the Four Agreements

7

A Dialogue with don Miguel

The Four Agreements were created to assist you in the Art of Transformation, to help you break the limiting agreements, gain more personal power, and become stronger.

THE FOUR AGREEMENTS

Question: You say that practicing the Four Agreements is the best way to make a transformation in your life. If we are using these tools and practicing the Four Agreements, what if something doesn't happen?

don Miguel: If you do it, it will happen. If you practice, it happens.

Question: If we follow the Four Agreements, what signs will show us that we are changing?

don Miguel: First, you will see changes in your personal life, in the way you feel about yourself, including changes in the way you judge yourself, the way you carry your guilt, your shame, your anger, your jealousy. You can measure your progress by your own happiness. If you are happy, if you feel good about yourself, that means you have improved a lot. You can see progress when you are no longer afraid to say the truth, when you can say, "I want this instead of that," or when you no longer say, "Why even try? It will never work; I always lose."

Of course, you will need mirrors to see yourself also, and the best kind of mirrors are the people who challenge you. An example: You have a problem with your boss at work, and the situation may be the same as before, but now you see less drama in your reaction; you react less to other people's points of view, to other people's poison. You are happy in your world, even with that boss.

The challenges in life help you to measure your progress. If you don't have challenges, how do you know if you are evolving? It's the action–reaction that makes the difference. It is not about mentally saying, "I know that." Who cares if you know or don't know something? What is more important is to take the action, to be alive, to be yourself.

....

Question: When I first read *The Four Agreements*, I was so excited about using these principles in my life. But now I look around and see the people around me living in their own hells, and it's discouraging. How do I keep my enthusiasm when I am surrounded by so many people who are in an old dream?

don Miguel: If you know the Four Agreements, by now you know that you don't have to take personally the way other people dream; you know that their dream has nothing to do with you. But if you really want to help other people, you can share the Four Agreements with them. If they know your personal mythology, and if they agree with you, very soon you can share that awareness, and have agreements to support one another. But if they don't have the awareness, they never will try to change, and it's not up to you to try to change them.

....

Question: Are there any belief systems that the Four Agreements are not compatible with? I was raised in a very religious family. Do I need to abandon my religion to follow the Four Agreements, or is there a way to incorporate them into my religion?

don Miguel: It doesn't matter what religion or philosophy you have; the Four Agreements can be applied by anyone, in any religion or in any philosophy in the world. The messenger is completely neutral; it is not giving you a philosophy or a religion to follow. It is not telling you how to live your life if you want to be safe or don't want to be condemned. The information can go in many different directions because it's based on awareness; it's based on common sense.

The Four Agreements can be used to help you raise your children, to improve the relationship with your beloved, your parents, anyone. They can help you to explore and adopt alternative beliefs, but you will transform your dream in your way, not mine. I am not interested in changing your concepts or beliefs; this is up to you. Imposing our will on others only creates more dogmas, more separation, more excuses for war. This is not what we want. We want to be happy, we want to be ourselves, and this is a very simple way.

Question: The Four Agreements have helped me so much. I would love to be involved in helping children learn these agreements so they can avoid a lot of the suffering most adults have gone through. Do you have any thoughts on this?

don Miguel: Someone recently asked me, "Miguel, why don't you work with children?" And my answer was, "They have parents." The answer is to work with the parents and to work with the teachers to apply the

Four Agreements. Then the adults will domesticate the children in a different way.

There is a program starting in Colorado that will share the Four Agreements with parents and teachers, who will work together to introduce it to the children. If this program works, then it will spread to other schools. If we domesticate our children with a different kind of knowledge, both at home and at school, a new generation of people will take control of the whole society in the future. The whole dream will change even faster.

BELIEFS AND AGREEMENTS

We didn't choose these beliefs, and we may have rebelled against them, but we were not strong enough to win the rebellion. The result is surrender to the beliefs with our agreement.

Question: When we try to change our beliefs, and we say to ourselves, "I am beautiful, I am smart," aren't these still beliefs that we are just choosing to make us happy?

don Miguel: Whatever you believe is still a belief. It doesn't matter if it is true. To be beautiful or to be ugly is just a point of view. To be smart or stupid, right or wrong, is just a concept. Neither is true. Either way, it is just a concept, it is just a dream.

What we find out is that every action has a reaction. If I look at myself in the mirror and say, "I look ugly," that is going to make me feel bad. But if I look in the mirror and say, "I look beautiful," then I'm going to feel good. It doesn't matter if it's true; it's just a choice. You choose happiness or you choose to suffer — that is the whole point.

Response: Mostly I find myself saying the same thing over and over again, even when it makes me suffer.

don Miguel: If we cannot stop suffering even if the reasoning mind says, "I don't want to suffer," it's because it isn't the reasoning mind that makes the choices; it's the belief system; it's the program. You can try to lie to yourself and say, "Yes, I believe I am beautiful," but deep inside, you believe that you are not beautiful. The belief is what you have to change — not what you want to believe, but what you *really* believe.

Everything is stored in the mind by agreement, and if you believe that agreement without a doubt, your faith is there. If an agreement is strong, it is because you have practiced it all your life, and it becomes automatic, without thinking. The reasoning mind can say "I believe," but it's lying to you. The only way to break an agreement is to replace it with another agreement, and to practice exactly the opposite. Practice makes the master.

Question: When you broke the structure of your beliefs, do you mean that you no longer have a structure, or do you mean that you keep building a new belief system?

don Miguel: I am like water, which is formless. Water takes form according to the container, and I change according to what I need in the moment. If I don't need structure, just like water I adjust to whatever is.

But if I do need structure, I create the structure, and use the structure. For me, all the knowledge of humanity is mythology, and it's beautiful. Knowledge is just the description of a dream; it is just a tool of communication that is in my pocket. I use it to speak the same language, and I can use language to go in any direction from sports to science, and to speak about almost anything and make sense about things that have no sense. But I hardly use the reasoning mind to talk to myself anymore; I just open myself to feel and to perceive. Those who know me in my private life will see that I am very quiet. I don't talk too much because I hardly have anything to say. But at a certain point when I have to, I create a whole structure and I speak the same language as everybody else. I know it is acting; it is just controlled folly, but I enjoy it.

Question: Why bother creating a new structure, a new belief system, if it's all just beliefs and not really the truth?

don Miguel: To change your beliefs is your personal choice. You don't have to change your beliefs or change your dream, or do anything at all. You can live your life in drama; you don't have to stop suffering, or stop your anger or your jealousy or your shame. You don't have to stop your self-abuse or stop punishing your-self, or stop all those disagreements you have with the people you love. You don't have to stop being what you are. But there is a better way to do it.

It's not that you have to change your beliefs. It's a choice; it's there, and it's been there for thousands of years. It's nothing new. Buddha taught us how to do it; Jesus taught us how to do it. Many other teachers around the world have said the same thing. They discovered a better way to be, a better way to interact with one another, and they shared it with others.

I would never tell you that you have to change; I only tell you that there is another way. You can take it, or you can leave it. But to love is a choice also, and that's the point; there is another way.

PARASITES

From the Toltec point of view, all humans who are domesticated are sick. They are sick because there is a Parasite that controls the mind and controls the brain. The food for the Parasite is the negative emotions that come from fear.

Question: I always thought Parasites were an important part of life. If I look at my own life, I don't think Parasites are the problem, but rather my reaction to Parasites is the problem. I'm stuck because I hear you saying that Parasites are always negative, but I don't know if that's true.

don Miguel: By definition, a Parasite is a living being who lives off you, with no benefit to you. From our point of view we can say that Parasites are evil, but this is only our point of view. To those Parasites we are just food; it's nothing personal. Those Parasites see the humans as we see the chickens, the cows, and the fruit trees. Yes, we put all those cows together in a pasture, and it looks like we are taking care of them, but we will kill them to eat the meat. It looks like the Parasite takes care of us also, but this is not true.

What Toltec mythology calls a Parasite refers to a living being that is living through people and eating them alive. By taking life from those people, it is destroying them, in many cases even killing them, as in suicide or addiction to drugs. Parasites lead people to self-destruction.

Knowledge, or thought forms that don't destroy you, that give you more life instead of taking life away from you, are no longer Parasites. Then we can call it a symbiotic interaction, which is completely different. The Toltec call these beings allies. In many traditions in the past, they called them gods.

In the Toltec tradition, if you face the Parasite and win the war against the Parasite, then the Parasite becomes your ally. It is no longer destroying you, but is facilitating what you do. If you have all those beliefs that go against you, you break the agreement, you shift it, and now the new belief will facilitate your creation, your happiness, your love. Knowledge becomes your ally; it is no longer your enemy. As I have said before, knowledge is not good or bad or right or wrong; it is the Parasite that contaminates knowledge that we can call evil.

Question: If we are here to have fun and be happy, why can't we enjoy our Parasite?

don Miguel: If you learn to make fun of yourself, you will enjoy your Parasite, and by making fun of your Parasite, you take a big step toward breaking many agreements. Nothing in the entire world is serious.

Question: Wouldn't it be boring to live a life with no drama, no sadness, and no suffering?

don Miguel: No! You can have drama and sadness and still have a boring life. What makes you bored is inaction. Boredom has nothing to do with the Parasite. The Parasite can keep you crying and very occupied. You can cry so much that you get bored, or you can laugh so much that you get bored. It doesn't matter if you are in heaven or in hell, if you don't have action, if you decide not to participate in life, you are going to be bored. It is our nature to create. Just like our creator, we love to create, and if we are doing that we don't get bored.

....

Question: Aren't we going to suffer anyway because we're human?

don Miguel: Many times when we suffer we say, "Well, it's because we are human." The concept of human in this society has a lot of limitations. The concept of "human" is a belief, it's just a concept, and the belief is that a lot of things cannot be possible. Humans have the need to know, and we suffer because we know what we believe. What do we believe? That's the big problem. Humans divide everything into duality: good and bad, right and wrong, beautiful and ugly. We have a need to be right about what we believe, even though it's not the truth. Knowing that we are not what we pretend to be or what we want to be, makes us suffer, feel shame, and reject ourselves.

Suffering is a habit, an addiction like any other, but more powerful. Imagine how difficult it is to stop smoking, and it is a thousand times more difficult to break the addiction to suffering. Suffering comes from the agreements we created. We suffer because we know our agreements. Then we become attached to suffering because we know suffering so well; it makes us feel safe. To change the dream, we need to change the agreements.

Question: You have said that truth restores our integrity and sets us free from the lies we believe, but how do we know whether we are going against the Parasite or going against our own integrity?

don Miguel: This is the tricky part because the belief system that breaks our integrity has our loyalty, and when we go against the belief system, it looks like we are going against ourselves. To see the truth is extremely difficult, but what is easier to see is what is not the truth.

Response: But how do you see it when you're in that position?

don Miguel: Well, first a couple of rules. Don't believe yourself, and don't believe anybody else. If you don't believe, what is not true will dissolve in front of your eyes. Only what is true will remain because what is true doesn't need anybody to believe it. Also, go inside and listen to your body, because your body will never lie to you. Your mind will play tricks, but the way you feel in your heart, in your guts, is the truth.

....

Question: If we start to use the truth with our children, can we inoculate them from the Parasite?

don Miguel: Children are going to have their own Parasites because each child is going to be domesticated. Domestication is not a bad thing; it just is. And if you do not domesticate your children, someone else will.

It's better that you domesticate them not to believe other people's opinions, and always to listen to their own truth. This will help them when they grow up to fight against their own Parasite.

Children live their own lives. You can only do your best to teach them responsibility for their agreements, and that action is your love for the child.

......

Question: When you talk about Parasites eating our emotions or humans using black magic, isn't this just mythology?

don Miguel: Yes, it's just mythology. In all the different cultures, it has always been a challenge to put this information into words. The story of Adam and Eve with the evil serpent, for example, makes it easier to explain what happens when we eat knowledge. Through the story, we can create an image and send that image to others. The kind of mythology we use to explain why we suffer just depends on how we use our imagination. In the Toltec tradition, we talk about the allies. When I say that humans are the best black magicians because we use our word to put spells on ourselves, it's just mythology. It's not really black magic that we use. The truth is that it's simply action—reaction. We learn, we believe; that is our curse.

In *The Four Agreements*, I have tried to take away most of the mythology and superstition, and keep the common sense. I only share four agreements to make it as simple as possible. If we use as little knowledge as possible, it is better for us.

Question: Will there ever come a time when humanity is living without Parasites?

don Miguel: I have no doubt that it will happen. Humanity is going in that direction. The whole big Parasite will shift into an ally and become a whole new dream. Even if we resist, it is going to happen around the world. We will not destroy ourselves. That is what the Parasite wants, but the Parasite is our creation, and that makes us more powerful than it is.

If you look at the last seven or eight hundred years, you can see how the dream is evolving. The way we dream now is very different from the way we dreamed even one hundred years ago. If you imagine yourself living that dream of eight hundred years ago, the dream you have right now is heaven compared with that dream. Even compared to the king, or the priest, or the pope of that time, you are in heaven.

Now imagine someone coming from seven or eight hundred years in the future, from the most advanced society of that time, and she sees the way you dream your life and sees the whole society you live in. Can you see the evolution of the dream, the direction it is going? Compared with the past, this is heaven. Compared with the future, this is hell.

So there is a healing process happening in the world. In the interaction between the dream and the dreamer, the whole humanity is evolving as one living being. This is because new dreamers with enough power send their dream to the outside dream and start modifying the dream.

If we have awareness, we are going to change the dream, and be Parasite-free. And we are doing it; that is the good part. If I can do it, you can do it. If you can do it, the whole world can do it. It can happen for all of us. The only thing we have to do is heal the dreamer: heal our personal importance, heal our own mind, and take our place in our own way.

....

Question: Is there something we can do to facilitate the healing process?

don Miguel: You only have to be who you really are. Our natural state is to love and be happy. It is easy to be happy. It is easy to enjoy life. It is easy to make fun of everything. It is easy to always live in a romance with life. You don't have to follow any tradition, you don't have to follow any dogma. It is not about acquiring more knowledge or mental concepts; it is about being alive. The mission each one of you have is to be happy and that is all. With awareness and action, you can break your own domestication, and live your life based in love instead of fear. With practice, you can become a dream master and transform your entire dream.

Question: So our mission is to be happy and not to add poison?

don Miguel: That is a choice. It took me a long time not to add poison. It took a lot of awareness, a lot of practice, because I had mastered the opposite. You know, all the poison I used to spread was because I had practiced spreading poison. I then practiced the opposite until I mastered it. Action–reaction: If you cut your finger, it hurts; but if you keep it clean it will not get infected. Cleaning the body is a habit. Not to take anything personally, and not to make assumptions are also habits.

Question: When you say "I," do you mean your body or your mind?

don Miguel: The answer is I don't know. But I know that I am alive and I am here. Then whoever is here is the one who answered your question.

....

Question: You say your mission is to be happy, but what do you do when someone you love dies, or you lose your job, or you lose your health?

don Miguel: Well, those things are going to hurt, and while it hurts I may not be happy. But it is not my choice that my loved one dies; I don't choose to lose my job. I don't choose to have cancer or to have the flu, but it happens because this body is alive. Anything can happen to this body. If I am here, I can be hurt by people's poison. I can be crucified, I can be shot, or someone can beat me up. If I am in the jungle, I can be bitten by a snake, or a tiger can get me. I am here, and I am exposed to life like everybody else.

The only difference will be that I will not take it personally. If I can avoid it, I will avoid it; it will not be my choice. If my mother dies, of course that will hurt. If I cut my finger, that will hurt too. But I will not contaminate it with poison. I will not try to justify it or blame anybody. I will not say, "Oh God, why did you take my mother?" Why even bother? Or if my wife leaves me, God bless her. I will not ask her, "What did I do to make you leave me? Give me a reason why." Whatever she says can only be used against myself. I don't need to understand why. If she wants to go, God bless her, and bye-bye.

BE IMPECCABLE WITH YOUR WORD

All the magic you possess is based on your word. Depending upon how it is used, the word can set you free, or it can enslave you even more than you know.

Question: If someone asks me what I think about someone else, and I tell the truth, I feel like I'm gossiping. If I don't tell the truth, then I'm lying to that person. What should I do?

don Miguel: Just don't give any information. It's the same advice as my grandfather used to give me: "Don't put your nose where nobody wants it." Just say, "I have no opinion" or "It's not my business."

....

Question: Does being impeccable mean that you always tell the truth, even when it hurts someone's feelings? How can I be impeccable without damaging my relationships or hurting others?

don Miguel: Well, you are also impeccable when you don't put your nose where nobody wants it. You don't have the right to try to fix other people's points of view. You don't need to be right and make them wrong because of what you believe. They have the right to suffer if that's what they want to do. Many times, people don't want you to tell them the truth; they only want you to tell them what they want to hear. You have to be wise enough to understand that when they ask you something, they are expecting a certain answer. You can go along with the game or not; it's up to you. But you don't need to create a lot of enemies by telling them what you think is true. That is not what they want to hear.

Again, it's just common sense. You can avoid the question, or you can tell them that you don't have any opinion about that. The problem is that they can take your words and change your words, and use them for gossiping. Many people only want your point of view to get evidence of what they believe about themselves or about someone else. They will come to you and ask, "What is your opinion? What do you think about this or that?" and you can give your sincere opinion, but they will change it. And then they will say that *you* said that about them, and involve you in gossip.

This reminds me of another thing my grandfather used to tell me. He said, "When you know you are going to make a mistake, shut your mouth; and if you already made a mistake, shut your mouth even tighter." Don't even try to fix it; you can only make it worse because people will change everything you say.

Sometimes you give information to your friends because you trust them and believe they are loyal to you. Maybe it's your best friend, and you gossip about yourself and tell her what you feel about yourself, about other people, making the assumption that she will not share it with anybody. And perhaps this is true, until she is no longer your friend. If something happens and she gets hurt or angry and breaks the friendship with you, a way for her to get even with you is to gossip about all the information you gave her. Something you have to learn about gossiping is that it begins with yourself. Don't gossip about yourself.

Question: If I have a relationship with someone who is not a good communicator or who doesn't like to communicate with me, how do I establish good communication?

don Miguel: If someone doesn't want to listen to you, why do you have to waste your time trying to talk to that person? If the person wants to hear what you have to say, he is going to try to use his attention to understand you. But if he doesn't want to even pay attention to you, why do you have to bother spending your time with that person? It's not really your problem.

One thing I used to teach my apprentices is to practice communicating to a wall. A wall doesn't react, and you don't expect it to understand what you're trying to say. You look for many ways to say the same thing, and by practicing in this way, your communication skills become stronger. Then if it's really important to you that this person understands you, you're going to look for all the different ways to communicate what you want to say. And if that person doesn't understand your communication, it's not up to you. You did your best; you don't have to worry about that anymore.

Response: Okay, but what if someone is willing to communicate but doesn't know how to express his feelings? Is there something I can do to help him communicate?

don Miguel: Well, just let that person know that he has your full attention, that you are willing to listen, that you are willing to communicate. You invite him to communicate, but you cannot force him to communicate.

If that person is very important to you — if it's your own child, or your mother, your spouse, your sister, someone whose presence you cannot avoid — then you can make yourself available to communicate. But if that person doesn't want to communicate, just accept him the way he is. And if it's someone you really don't need to be around, then you don't have to be around that person, because it's not fun really if there's no communication.

Question: When someone is gossiping, what is the most tactful way of stopping the gossip?

don Miguel: The best way to stop others from gossiping is by not reacting to their gossip. If you react, you encourage them to gossip even more. If you don't react, and they see that it's not affecting you, at a certain point they just let it go. If you don't accept the poison they send, that poison doesn't affect you.

Question: I have difficulty knowing how to tell my friends and co-workers that I don't want to gossip anymore. I have tried to make an agreement with my best friend not to gossip, but she still gossips. How can I keep my agreement not to gossip without looking arrogant and losing my friends?

don Miguel: While you are breaking your agreements, you will be dealing with people who are not involved in this process and you have no control over them. Their behavior is the result of their beliefs and their wounds. What they do about it is not up to you; they are not your business or your problem. All you can do is work to change your agreements with yourself, and the agreements that you make with other people. The agreements with other people have two sides, and each person is responsible for his half only. If you make an agreement with someone and they break the agreement, you need to make another agreement if you want to remain in a relationship with that person. You are lying to yourself if you pretend the agreement is still in place.

If that person is not keeping her word, it's up to you to stay there or not, according to your personal integrity.

Question: If I am talking to a friend of mine about another person we both know, does this mean I am gossiping even if I don't say anything bad about that person?

don Miguel: Gossiping can have good intentions, bad intentions, or no intentions at all. But even when the originator of the gossip doesn't have a bad intention, the receiver of the information can change it into a bad intention. Whoever hears the information digests the information, and then changes it according to his or her perception.

Whatever you tell people can also be used by their Parasite. Their Parasite will change and manipulate the information you give them according to their point of view. That's why it's better not to gossip at all.

Question: What if you are trying to live your life with impeccability of the word, and you have a child who because of society or their friends or school, grows up to not be impeccable with her word? Of course I want my child to be impeccable. What would you do about this?

don Miguel: Because I love my children, I want them to be whatever they are going to be.

Response: Whether or not they are happy?

don Miguel: Their happiness is not up to me; it is up to them. It is not my love that will make them happy, it is their love that will make them happy.

Question: Self-love is a concept that is hard for me to grasp. Where do I start with that?

don Miguel: Start by accepting who you are, as you are right now, even though you know you are not perfect according to your image of perfection. It's always easier to start with self-acceptance.

When I discovered that I was mentally sick, that I had a Parasite in my head, of course I rebelled against the Parasite, but I accepted myself just the way I am: an angel with a Parasite. I now see it is okay to be sick. It is not wrong to be sick. A mental disease is like any other disease: You will not judge yourself because you have the flu. We have a disease with a Parasite in our head. You don't take it personally, of course. But once you know about the Parasite, you want to be healed. You want to heal your flu not because you think you are bad because you have the flu. You are not guilty because you have the flu. You just don't want to have the flu.

If you don't accept yourself, you are really rejecting yourself. Then because we make the assumption that other people believe what we believe and feel what we feel, we make the assumption that other people will reject us for the same reasons we reject ourselves. Before other people can reject us, we reject ourselves. Once you accept yourself, you also make the assumption that others accept you as you are. The whole cycle of action–reaction is broken just by accepting yourself the way you are.

....

Question: Whenever I start to think about improving myself, I get confused because then I'm not accepting myself exactly as I am. How can I accept myself exactly as I am and still try to improve myself?

don Miguel: You can be aware that you want to improve yourself, but not because you believe you are not good enough. It is possible to improve yourself without rejecting yourself.

Let's say that you are unaware of your emotional reactions for a long time. Then finally for whatever reason, you are aware of your emotional reactions. Before you were aware of them, you used to judge yourself and punish yourself for having those reactions. With awareness you find out that those reactions were how you practiced being yourself. But just because you know this doesn't mean you will stop having those reactions. As soon as you accept yourself, even if you have those reactions, you no longer judge yourself the way you did before. Just like magic, if you accept yourself the way you are with your reactions, you don't judge yourself or find yourself guilty for having those reactions. If you don't find yourself guilty, you will not punish yourself. You are not adding more drama to your reactions. As soon as you accept yourself, right away things start changing for the better. By having the awareness and not judging yourself, you have already improved.

If we judge ourselves because we have a Parasite, we are giving more power to the Parasite. Remember, the Parasite is very clever; the Parasite makes a proposition, and the Parasite accepts it. When the Parasite is discovered, it will say, "I don't want to have the Parasite anymore. Let's get rid of the Parasite." And we agree with it. Do you understand the trick? That is the Parasite who is speaking, and the Parasite who is listening at the same time. The Parasite says, "Okay, let's rebel," and we say, "I am going to be a great spiritual warrior." Later the Parasite will say: "What kind of warrior am I? I still take things personally, I still make assumptions." It is because the Parasite makes the proposition and the Parasite agrees to it.

It is the Parasite who is thinking, thinking, thinking. Where are you? That snake in the Tree of Knowledge is really a genius. It took possession of all of us. Once we accept ourselves — okay, we have a Parasite — no problem. We don't play the game of the Parasite. We learn to control the emotions; and when we control the emotions, we don't feed the Parasite anymore. The only way to control the emotions is by accepting ourselves just the way we are. When we learn to make fun of ourselves, we start behaving in a way that the Parasite is not expecting. Of course, the Parasite will then try to propose an agreement and accept it about making fun of ourselves. That's why the Toltecs teach us how to be hunters, how to be aware of what the Parasite is doing. Because the Parasite is always hunting us, we must learn to hunt the Parasite.

Don't take anything personally

All people live in their own dream, in their own mind; they are in a completely different world from the one we live in. Even when a situation seems so personal, even if others insult you directly, it has nothing to do with you.

Question: The second agreement, "Don't take anything personally," is the agreement I really want to master in my life, but I can't see how someone's criticism of me is not personal. If my friend or my boss says something that really hurts my feelings, how can you say this isn't personal or that it's not about me?

don Miguel: I want you to imagine that one day you awake in France or Italy seven or eight hundred years ago. You understand the language very well, but you are going to see that society from the point of view that you have right now, with all that you know right now, with all the beliefs you have about yourself, about society, about science, psychology, sociology, everything.

I want you to imagine the way people treat one another in France or Italy during the Middle Ages.

Imagine what they believe about everything — about religion, death, science, medicine. There are people who don't bathe for months because it is a sin. Imagine the moral judgments of that society: what is right, what is wrong, what they *believe* is right or wrong. Imagine what it would mean to be a woman then, with the mentality of the present time. If you start a romantic relationship, how are you going to deal with that relationship? Put yourself in that place, just for a moment.

What are you going to do when the people in that society start judging you? You could be the greatest teacher in that society, you could be a great angel or messenger for those people, and they may kill you because of your beliefs. If you know that they can kill you for what you believe, how are you going to deal with them?

Knowing what you know, and knowing what they believe, the way they dream, are you really going to make assumptions? Are you really going to take personally what they say to you, what they believe, the way they judge you? Are you going to feel emotionally hurt for the judgments they have about you when you know the way they dream? It is silly to even think that you are going to take it personally. It is silly to think that you are going to feel emotionally hurt because they judge you.

Response: Well, I guess that's true, but I would also understand that these people have a different worldview.

don Miguel: Everybody you meet has a different worldview, even now. Imagine your boss at work with those beliefs of eight hundred years ago. With the way you think right now, you will not even suffer because whatever tantrum the boss has is not going to affect you. It is going to be funny. Of course you will refrain from laughing because that could have dire consequences. Laugh about the priests eight hundred years ago, and you were dead. Then you had to learn not to laugh at them.

It's the same thing now. It's simply that people have different points of view. You know, the behavior of other people's Parasites is funny. Believe me, I could laugh if it was not so dramatic at the same time. One of the things I always suggest is to learn to make fun of yourself. If you learn to make fun of yourself every time your Parasite gets you, or another person's Parasite gets you, then instead of judging yourself or judging that person, you are going to have a great time. Of course, when you deal with sick people, you are going to reflect them, that's all. But it's going to be funny to see every reaction of your Parasite.

Response: Okay. I get it now. Still, it's going to be a challenge to think it's funny when someone is putting me down or yelling at me.

don Miguel: Many of the funniest things that happen in our lives don't look funny when they are happening. Later we can laugh, but at that time we are possessed by our Parasite, which means our mental disease is having a crisis.

When the anger comes out and overtakes us, the Parasite is obvious because of the crisis, but even when we don't feel the Parasite, it doesn't mean our mind is healed. We may not have a crisis right now, but the Parasite is there, waiting for the moment to come out. It comes out when we have a crisis, and the crisis can manifest in different ways, but we look like the little girl in the movie *The Exorcist* who is possessed by demons.

When I awoke from the dream of the planet, what I discovered is that everybody around me is possessed just like the little girl in that movie. But they don't know it because it's normal behavior for them. People are possessed and what possesses them is so amazing to see. The Parasite is living their life. The big Parasite is made up of all those teeny, tiny Parasites that eat our emotions. I call them garbage eaters because they eat garbage from my point of view.

The next time you get angry, or jealous, or sad, put a mirror in front of your face and see your expression; compare your face with the little girl in the movie. Who is behind that face? It is nothing to be afraid of; you don't need to start praying right away. You have been like that all your life and it hasn't destroyed you. The Parasite has already tried its best to destroy you, so it cannot get worse than that, it can only get better. Just remember this: any time you see any human in anger, any time you see the envy or the jealousy of someone, he or she is possessed. It is nothing personal.

....

Question: I am doing my best not to take anything personally. I understand that it's not about me, but when people criticize me or say something hurtful, I still feel really awful. What am I doing wrong?

don Miguel: There is nothing you are doing wrong. You feel like that because you believe what they say, because you align your beliefs with them. What someone says will only affect you if you believe it.

Imagine that you are a child, and you make a little mistake that angers your father. You don't even know what the mistake is, but your father is angry and says, "You are a stupid child; you should feel ashamed of yourself." You agree with your father, and put your faith in that agreement; you believe it 100 percent without a doubt.

You grow up and now you say, "I am intelligent; it's not true that I'm stupid." But when someone comes and says, "What you did was stupid; you should be ashamed of yourself," you react right away with anger and it's because you believe what that person said. You kept that knowledge in your head, the agreement that it's true that you are stupid. Later, when someone touches that little splinter, the reaction is a lot of emotional pain. But if you don't believe what he says, you don't react. You are going to laugh.

If you believe you are worth it, and someone says, "You don't deserve that," it doesn't affect you because you don't believe it. You agreed that you are worth it, so you just laugh about it, and say, "Oh sure," but you don't believe it. And because you don't believe it, it will not affect you.

Don't make assumptions

We have the tendency to make assumptions about everything. The problem with making assumptions is that we believe they are the

*truth. We make an assumption, we misunderstand, we take it
personally, and we end up creating a whole big drama for nothing.*

Question: How does a person stop making assumptions? My mind goes off and starts to think of all these things, and then I suffer all the time for no good reason.

don Miguel: The problem is that you think too much. You are way too smart. Think, think, think. Your mind is like a wild horse that takes you wherever it wants to take you. You have no control over all that thinking, all those assumptions — not just one assumption, a whole universe of assumptions. You think too much. Why do you need to think at all? Something I teach my apprentices is to become a master of thinking.

For me thinking is a tool for communication. I hardly think. For hours I just don't think, and not because I'm stupid. I don't think because I have no need to think. What I know, I know. I'm full of knowledge, but why do I need to think about what I know? Thinking, thinking, thinking: What is she doing? What is he doing? What about this? What about that? What if this happens? What if that happens?

Just thinking *"What if?"* creates a huge drama in our life. Every human can think a lot, and thinking brings fear. It's two o'clock in the morning, and you are still thinking, thinking, thinking. You need to tame the horse, and learn to ride the horse. The horse has to obey you and take you where you want to go.

You know, there is an impeccable way of thinking. If you have a problem, it's time to think. Once you make a choice about how to resolve the problem, it's time to stop thinking and take action. Now you know the solution; it's over. But guess what? You have a problem, you think of the solution, and you don't stop thinking. You're still thinking, and you find another solution, and you still don't stop. You keep thinking, and you come up with another solution.

If you have just one solution, you have all the power of intent and you can resolve it. If you have two solutions, you divide intent in two. Three solutions — you're losing power. Soon you're confused, and you have to think about which of the solutions is the best. When you feel confused you feel powerless, and you need someone else to tell you what to do. Making assumptions is all about thinking. If you just stop thinking, you no longer make assumptions. You need to learn to tame the horse.

....

Question: My question is about knowledge and assumptions. I was wondering if the voices I hear in my head and what you call "knowledge" are the same as assumptions?

don Miguel: What is an assumption?

Response: In my case, it's thinking that I know, so it's knowledge. Okay, you answered it.

don Miguel: We can divide everything into what we know, which is the known; what we don't know, which is the unknown; and what we will never know, which is the unknowable. We only know what we know: our knowledge. We only know the information accumulated in our mind by agreements. We know the whole reality that we perceive, we know our dream, we know our point of view.

The unknown is another story. Do you see the woman sitting next to you? You create an image and project it on her. You only know about her what you project, and this is the known for you. But what she has in her mind is unknown. You can make the assumption that you know what she has in her mind. You can make the assumption that you know your children, or your father, or your mother, or even your dog, but you don't know them. You only know what you believe about them; and it's only true for you, no one else, because it's your dream. The truth is that you will never know them. You hardly know yourself, but you pretend to know other people.

You only know what your knowledge tells you. You only know the judgments that you can make about everybody, the interpretations, your personal point of view. You don't know what other people feel, what they think, what they believe, what they are dreaming. And you make the assumption that they believe what you believe, that they feel what you feel, that they see the world the way you see the world. And it's knowledge that controls you.

As I said before, if we control knowledge, it becomes a tool of communication. We don't make assumptions, we ask. We ask, and other people will tell us what is in their world. Then we know what they have in their dream, they can communicate. It's that simple. We don't have to make assumptions, but we also know that they will tell us what *they* know. It doesn't mean it's true.

Response: Now I really see how making assumptions causes a lot of misunderstandings between people.

don Miguel: Even if we don't make assumptions, it's easy to see why humans hardly understand one another. People send us a distorted image of themselves, because it's only what they want to project to us, then we perceive the distorted image they send, and we distort it even more with our own beliefs. This is just the way it is. That's the way humans dream; the way we interact with one another. People project the image of their dream to us, and we distort it according to what we want to believe. We have to make everything we perceive fit into what we already believe, just to be sure that what we believe is true. That's why we are more interested in hooking the attention of other people to project our point of view than in listening to what other people want to say to us.

ALWAYS DO YOUR BEST

In your everyday moods your best can change from one moment to another, from one hour to the next, from one day to another. Your best will also change over time. As you build the habit of the four new agreements, your best will become better than it used to be.

Question: I always try to do my best, but what should I do when someone asks me to do something that I don't want to do or that I'm too tired to do? How do I do my best when I am exhausted or just need time for myself? I feel like I'm always disappointing myself or someone else.

don Miguel: First, you have to be honest with yourself and see if you want to do whatever someone is asking of you. If you don't want to do it, and you have the opportunity of not doing it, just be honest and find the easiest way to say, "I will not do it." Sometimes, of course, this is not possible. You might have a contract with someone, or feel you have to do it because you know it's going to help you in your life.

Then instead of believing that you don't want to do it, it's up to you to change your belief, create desire, and do it. Use your reason, your knowledge, to talk to yourself and say, "Yes, I want to do it," and tell yourself why it's good for you to do it, even if you really don't want to do it. In that moment you will do your best, but first you have to change your mind, change the action, because whatever you do, there will be a reaction.

If there is something you don't like to do, and avoiding it will only cause a bigger problem for you, then you're not really being impeccable. If you have a problem, even if you don't want to face it, it is better to face the problem, whatever it is, and do your best. Once you have done that, you don't have to worry about it anymore.

....

Question: I have been taking care of other people my entire life. Recently, I decided to put myself first and take care of some of my own needs. As soon as I decided this, the Judge came up and said, "No, no, no. You are being selfish; you should be taking care of everybody else." Well, that is how I've lived my life, and I've been totally empty.

don Miguel: People around you are used to you helping them and sacrificing yourself for them. They can ask you for whatever they want, and they know you will do it for them. Well, the day you stop doing that, what happens? Others will tell you that you are selfish. Who is really selfish? Are you, the martyr, the selfish one, or is the one who takes advantage of you the selfish one?

You no longer need to take care of other people, but you *believe* that you do; it is one of the agreements you have with yourself. You can break that agreement by doing exactly the opposite. By practicing the opposite, many other agreements that limit your freedom will go along with it.

....

Question: I have been doing my best to improve my life, but every time I start making progress and begin to feel happier, I fall right back into my old habits. Why is it such a struggle?

don Miguel: Because you believe what you know without a doubt, and whatever you believe is what rules your life. People believe 100 percent in what they believe they are. That is why they live their life the way they do. If you believe you are a loser, what is going to happen? Because you believe you are a loser, *thy will be done.* Your reasoning mind can say, "I want to be rich, I want to be healthy," but what you believe is not in your reason. What you believe is in your Book of Law, and your faith is trapped inside that book.

When you are a child and your mother says, "You are never going to learn to dance," if you agree with her, then that's it — you are never going to learn to dance. Even if your reasoning mind says, "I don't know why I can't learn to dance," it is because you really believe you cannot learn to dance. If you believe that you're not good at sports, then you're not good at sports. If you believe that you're not beautiful, then that's it — you don't feel beautiful. Those beliefs are the Parasites, and they are eating you alive. People are exactly what they believe they are because they have complete faith in what they believe. That faith is their word, and they are using the word in the wrong way: against themselves.

....

Question: I have always tried to do my best in everything I do, but after reading *The Four Agreements*, I realized that I do it because I'm looking for the approval of other people. Then if I don't get the approval, I feel victimized, or if my husband makes a critical comment, I feel discouraged and wonder, "What's the use?" Can you comment on this?

don Miguel: During our domestication, one of the most powerful agreements we make is the need for approval, and the result of that is amazing. Because of the need for approval, one opinion can lift us up or completely destroy us. Searching for approval becomes a big routine, and that is how the outside dream has power over humans and manipulates us like puppets. We have to ask other people for their opinions: "How do I look? Did I sound okay? How am I driving? Am I doing okay?"

We need the support and acceptance of others; we need to be good enough for someone else. We even need someone else to need us in order to feel like we have a reason to be alive. What people think about us is so important that we try to please everybody else, and leave ourselves until last.

Doing your best does not mean to try to be good enough for someone else. The fact is that you will never be good enough for someone else. The truth is that with all your agreements you will never be good enough for yourself either. No matter what you do it won't be right. You can try to do more than your best, but you could kill yourself trying to be the best. Your best is never good enough because you made those agreements with the Judge in your mind. And the agreement with your Victim is such that even if you try your best you are not good enough, you are not strong enough, you are not intelligent enough. There is no hope. You will never please the Judge who lives in your mind because that Judge is very strict, very strong, and very abusive.

There is only one way to silence the voice of the Judge, and that is to make new agreements with ourselves. If we are going to have agreements, let's have agreements that make us happy.

8

True Stories of Awareness and Transformation

In this chapter, people who have applied the Four Agreements share their experiences.

BE IMPECCABLE WITH YOUR WORD

Breaking the agreement to gossip at work

It has been difficult for me to break the gossip habit, especially at work. I have always used gossiping as a way of being included in conversations with others. Whenever someone gossiped about a manager or co-worker, I would automatically believe the gossip, and judge that person based on what I had heard about him, rather than on my own experience.

Since reading *The Four Agreements*, I remind myself not to believe what I am hearing when other people gossip. Mostly I make sure not to pass any gossip along. I let it stop with me, and I release it without believing it to be the truth. I focus on sharing love in tiny ways instead of trying to feel better about myself by gossiping about others.

No more bad news

I had been married to a man who always brought me the bad news at the end of each day. It didn't matter whether it was personal or global bad news; he would deposit it with me. I agreed, under the assumption of being a good wife, that it was my duty to receive this verbal garbage. I didn't know it at the time, but all this garbage I had agreed to receive was slowly poisoning me. Later we divorced, but remained close friends. Throughout the years he continued to bring me his gossip, but after reading *The Four Agreements*, I knew it was time for me to honor the first agreement. In a great act of personal power, I told my former husband that I was no longer available to accept the garbage he brought to me. I told him that if he could find some other way of communicating about the world I would be happy to listen, but I was no longer available for the poison. We don't talk much anymore, but I have much more joy and self-respect.

Being impeccable

The first agreement inspired me to observe my thoughts. Every time I had an impulse to speak, I would pay attention to the need behind the words. Often it was a need to be noticed, to gain someone's approval, or to show someone what I know. It was a painful process, because suddenly I could see how often I am not impeccable with my word.

Being impeccable with my word taught me to communicate with self-respect and love. I've learned to stop gossiping about myself and others. If I am having a bad day, I can say, "I'm having a bad day," but I don't blow it out of proportion. If someone around me is having a bad day, I don't take it personally, and I do my best to be impeccable with *my* word, even if I feel wounded by other people's words.

Being impeccable with my word has opened many doors for me. I have learned to speak my truth without all the drama I used to create. This allows me to experience deeper, more meaningful communication in my personal and professional relationships.

Using the word with children

The first agreement, *be impeccable with your word*, is helping me to be a better parent. I am more aware of the importance of communicating with my children with impeccability. One morning, I was frustrated and yelled at my daughter for taking so long to get dressed. I realized immediately that I had not been impeccable with my word because of my own fear of being late. I later bought her flowers and apologized for my harsh words, letting her know that I was having a difficult day. It felt good to share my feelings with her in a respectful way.

Using the word to judge

The first agreement made me realize how much time I spend either judging myself or judging someone else. I live my life in total judgment! I am so determined to reclaim the part of my mind that is simply running a program, that I have begun to track my thoughts by setting the alarm on my watch to go off every twenty minutes. Each time I hear the alarm, I take note of where my thoughts are: Am I judging? I keep a notebook to record my thoughts throughout the day.

At the end of the day, I look at the list of thoughts and ask myself, "Is this what I want to be thinking?" This simple technique makes me aware of my thoughts and helps me to change the way I use my word. It has also helped me to see if the thoughts I am thinking are truly my own or if they are simply the unconscious program that is running.

Constructive self-talk

One morning as I walked past a mirror, I turned and smiled at myself and said, "You look beautiful today. I love you." This was a profound turning point in my life. Until that day, I had always looked in the mirror and said, "I look fat. My hair doesn't look so good today. My skin looks awful!" To find myself finally saying something positive to myself was a huge triumph.

DON'T TAKE ANYTHING PERSONALLY

Healing the mother-daughter relationship

I have been engaged in a battle with my mother for most of my life. I have judged my mother and rejected her based upon those judgments, and I have used her to victimize myself. One day, as I was reading *The Four Agreements,* I began to see that by judging my mother and using the power of my word against her, I was not only punishing her, but also punishing myself.

I wanted to apply the Four Agreements in my relationship with my mother, so I began by carefully listening to what she said to me. Instead of instantly reacting like I usually did, I simply noticed when she said things that triggered a reaction in me. I found that by not taking what she said personally, I could see my own dream more clearly. I began to hear the critical voices inside me that reflected her voice. I became more aware of all the times when I treated myself with disrespect and cruelty. Each time I took responsibility for my own self-judgments, I slowly began to release my mother as the target of my abusive thoughts. I allowed myself to start believing that she really had done the best she could.

My relationship with my mother has changed dramatically. It hasn't healed entirely, but I now see her through eyes filled more with love than with judgment, and a heart that does not need to protect itself from her. I do the best I can each time I am with her. Some days are better than others, but as long as I remember the Four Agreements and apply them to each situation, I know that I am moving one step closer to the kind of life I want to live.

Not taking ourselves personally

I was daydreaming when I noticed that parts of my mind were running along without me. I was fascinated by all the voices in my mind. I would put my attention on a thought, it would shift, and I couldn't catch what the voice had been talking about!

Until that moment, I had always thought it was me who was doing all the thinking. I began to understand what don Miguel means by the Parasite. The Parasite thinks without me, and had me fooled all this time that it *was* me. My attention gets hooked, and most of the time the chatter is centered around a myriad of things that might go wrong in my life.

After reading *The Four Agreements*, I have pierced a hole or two in the belief that the Parasite is the real me. My work is to stretch those holes larger and larger each day until they are big enough to step through to the real me. Now I find it much easier not to take even my own thoughts and feelings personally because nine times out of ten, they aren't me.

The Judge and the Victim at work

I had a boss at work who was very judgmental. No matter what I did, she would find fault with it and make a point of correcting me in a very cynical way. I really struggled with this. I would go to work and ask myself, "Why am I letting myself be abused this way?"

I was ready to quit my job when I read *The Four Agreements.* What struck me the most was the term "spiritual warrior," and "the discipline to be ourselves, no matter what." I decided to use the situation to become a better "warrior," and began by making a commitment to always do my best.

Over the next couple of months, I discovered that I was constantly afraid of being judged. This actually allowed my boss to be judgmental; I was playing the role of the Victim, and she was playing the role of the Judge. I continued to react to her judgments, and in some ways it was more difficult because I was so aware of my reactions. I would get angry, or feel betrayed whenever she criticized my work.

One day my boss said something to me and the dream suddenly shattered. What I saw was a woman who was fiercely critical of herself. When I finally understood that she was living in her own dream, and I was living in mine, everything shifted for me. In her dream, her own self-judgments caused her to be judgmental toward me, but it had nothing to do with me. In that moment, I felt compassion for her, and I never again took anything she said personally.

Whenever she judged me, I looked at my work and decided for myself whether I had done my best. Even if I made a mistake, if I knew I had done my best, I would move on and correct the problem. Before, my Judge always agreed with her Judge, and I'd spend the day beating myself up emotionally.

I worked at this office for another year and even though my boss could still be judgmental, she started to change. She began to compliment me on my work! By having compassion for her Judge and putting my own Victim to rest, our relationship was transformed. All I had to do was change my agreements!

DON'T MAKE ASSUMPTIONS

Making assumptions at home

A minor incident with a new roommate showed me the problem with making assumptions. During the summer we agreed to turn on the air conditioning only when we were at home. For three days in a row I came home to find my roommate gone and the air conditioner on full blast. Of course, I made the assumption that my roommate had left it on. By the third day, I was furious and was planning to ask her to move out. I imagined confronting her, and having to find another roommate. I was worried that I might lose the house if I couldn't find someone else to share the rent.

Later my boyfriend discovered that the air conditioner had been preset to go on at a certain time by the previous tenants. I felt so foolish for blaming my roommate. I had made an assumption, didn't question my assumption, and put myself through many hours of emotional turmoil. If I had asked a simple question, I would have avoided a lot of suffering.

Making assumptions at work

Last month my boss called me and asked me to come into his office. I had no idea what he wanted, and my mind immediately went to the project proposal I had just written him. What if he didn't like it? I had been in a hurry at the end. I must have made a mistake. I really didn't do my best on the proposal. If I get fired, what will I tell my family? Maybe it is about that new person, and he wants to replace me. On and on the chatter went. Instead of waiting to find out what my boss wanted, I created a hundred disaster scenarios in my mind. It turned out he wanted to thank me for the extra effort I put into getting the proposal to him on time.

Making assumptions about ourselves

My friend Anna and I tend to make very different assumptions about ourselves. I tend to overestimate myself. I am constantly taking on new projects, assuming that I can fit them all in to my life, and end up having to disappoint people. My friend tends to underestimate herself. She is a very capable artist, but often turns down projects because she assumes she doesn't have the skill she needs.

Now before I take on a new project, I call Anna, and we discuss whether it is too large a project. She calls me when she is asked to do something she's not sure she can handle. We help each other ask the pointed questions that allow us to make clear decisions, instead of decisions based on assumptions.

Making assumptions about a handicap

I was born with no forearms, and small hands that come out just below my elbows. For me, learning not to take anything personally, and not to make assumptions was a revolution in my life.

I was raised to believe that my physical disabilities don't have to limit me, but it wasn't until I read *The Four Agreements* that I saw how many choices I had made based on assumptions and taking what other people said or did personally.

I had been struggling with career and money issues for a long time, living off my disability check and going to college. I asked myself, "If I do not make the assumption that I am limited in any way, what would I want to do?" I knew in my heart that I wanted to be financially independent, but I had always assumed this was impossible. Now I am studying to be an accountant. I have stopped taking other people's beliefs about having a disability personally. I know that is their dream. My dream is one of unlimited potential. I used to make the assumption that many doors were closed for me. Now I do my best in each moment, with no expectations of being rejected.

ALWAYS DO YOUR BEST

Taking action because you want to

As a manager of a restaurant, I was supposed to be the first one at work in the morning to open the doors. Every morning I scrambled out of the house, drove through traffic frustrated because I was late, and arrived just seconds before the rest of the staff arrived. Sometimes I didn't make it on time, and my Judge would really come down on me. I knew I was not doing my best. My choices were creating a lot of anxiety in my life, but I loathed the idea of getting up any earlier.

One day I asked myself, "How can I do my best in this situation?" I decided to make a new agreement with myself to get up an hour earlier. From that day on I actually enjoyed the time I spent driving to work. I would arrive a half-hour early, and make coffee for the staff. They would arrive to find me relaxed and happy to see them. Doing my best was a huge gift that I gave myself.

Doing your best — no more, and no less

"Always do your best" is my favorite agreement. I'm a perfectionist and tend to overachieve. I had always thought that doing my best meant giving 110 percent at all times. Because of this, I was exhausted and often resentful. I ran from task to task, afraid that I was not doing enough. Now I give my best, no more and no less. I've slowed down, and I take the time to savor my work and my relationships. Life is so much more enjoyable!

No guilt or blame

Always doing my best has helped to keep the Judge at bay. All I have to do is ask myself: "Was that really my best effort?" If the answer is yes, there's not a lot the Judge can say. My Judge is harsh, but even my Judge knows that a person can only do her best. If I make mistakes, I do my best to correct them, and if I do my best, then I have fewer mistakes to correct.

The Four Agreements at the office

One of our managers was constantly talking about the Four Agreements and encouraged us to try them. So a group of us decided to see what would happen if we agreed not to gossip, and not to make assumptions. When the gossip in the office decreased, all the drama did too! People began to ask questions to clarify any communication that was unclear. We stopped assuming that someone else would take care of what had to get done, or that no one would help us if we were overwhelmed. By using the Four Agreements as a team, we reminded each other to be aware, and everyone's productivity increased. The Four Agreements have completely transformed our work environment!

New agreements save a crumbling relationship

I devoured *The Four Agreements* in one afternoon, and when my husband came home I could not stop talking about the book. The next day he listened to the book on tape while commuting to work. When he got home we talked, maybe for the first time ever. We talked about the way we had been taking each other's comments personally; about all the assumptions we had both made about each other; and mostly, about not being impeccable with our word.

I had been speaking to my husband as an enemy. He had been thinking of me as the enemy and moving toward protecting himself from me. We made the decision to keep these Four Agreements alive in ourselves and in our relationship. Now my husband is no longer my enemy; he is my ally. Keeping these Four

Agreements transformed our life from one of conflict to one of companionship.

I also passed *The Four Agreements* on to a woman who works at a homeless shelter and was thrilled to find out that the staff was devouring the book as I had. One day she called in high drama, totally engulfed in "she said, he said," and all I had to say was "Why are you taking it personally?" The drama disappeared in a second.

My sister was ending a twenty-six-year marriage and was completely steeped in melodrama. I sent her *The Four Agreements*, and after reading the book only once, her relationship was transformed into one of respect, compassion, and amiable dissolution.

What I have learned is that my emotional pain is never about the other person. It's not about my spouse, my children, my parents, my friends, or the stranger in the grocery store. It's always and only about me. What-ever anyone else is thinking or doing is never about me; it's always about them. What an incredible relief!

The Book of Law

Just as a government has a book of law that rules the society's dream, our belief system is the Book of Law that rules our life. Whatever is in our Book of Law is our supreme truth. We base all of our judgments on this Book of Law, even if these judgments go against our own inner nature.

The Domestication of Humans

Humans are domesticated the same way we train a dog or other animal: through a system of punishment and reward. In human domestication, information from the outside dream is conveyed to the inside dream, creating our whole belief system, and teaching us how to be a human.

Dreaming

Dreaming is the main function of the mind, and the mind dreams twenty-four hours a day. When the brain is awake, there is a material frame that makes us perceive things in a linear way; when we go to sleep we do not have the frame, and the dream has the tendency to change constantly.

The Dream of the Planet

Society's dream, or the dream of the planet, is the collective dream of billions of personal dreams. Together these create a dream of a family, of a community, of a city, of a country, and finally a dream of all humanity. The dream of the planet includes all of society's rules, beliefs, laws, religions, governments, schools, and social customs. In this dream it is normal for humans to suffer; fear is an important part of this dream.

The Image of Perfection

During domestication, we form an image of perfection to please other people, to be good enough for them. But we are never perfect from this point of view, and so we begin to reject ourselves. The image of perfection is the reason we abuse ourselves; it is the reason we reject our own humanity. We also judge others according to our image of perfection, and they can never measure up to that ideal.

The Judge

The inner Judge uses what is in our Book of Law to judge everything we do, everything we think, and everything we feel. Every time we do something that goes against the Book of Law, the Judge says we are guilty, we should be ashamed, and we need to be punished.

Mitote

The Toltec use this term to refer to the condition of the human mind. The mitote can be compared to a huge marketplace where thousands of people are talking at the same time, and nobody understands each other. The mitote is also like a fog that blinds us from seeing the truth.

The Parasite

The Toltec compare the Judge, the Victim, and the belief system to a Parasite that invades the human mind. The Parasite is a living being made of psychic or emotional energy. It can also be compared to a program that dreams through our mind and lives through our body. From the Toltec point of view, all humans who are domesticated are sick because we have a Parasite that thrives on the emotions that come from fear and suffering.

Personal Importance

During the period of our domestication, we learn to think we are responsible for everything: "Me, me, always me." Personal importance, or taking things personally, is the maximum expression of selfishness because we make the assumption that everything is about "me."

The Victim

The Victim is the part of our mind that receives the judgments, and carries the blame, the guilt, and the shame. The Judge decrees, and the Victim suffers the guilt and punishment. The Victim is always crying, "Poor me" because of a deep sense of injustice: It doesn't matter what the Victim does to please the Judge, it is *never* good enough.

About the Authors

Don Miguel Ruiz is a master of the Toltec mystery school tradition. For more than two decades, he has worked to impart the wisdom of the ancient Toltec to a small group of students and apprentices, guiding them toward their personal freedom. Today, he continues to combine his unique blend of ancient wisdom and modern-day awareness through lectures, workshops, and journeys to sacred sites around the world.

For information about current programs offered
by don Miguel Ruiz and his apprentices,
please visit his web site at www.miguelruiz.com

≈

Janet Mills is the editor and publisher of Amber-Allen Publishing. She is the author of *The Power of a Woman* and *Free of Dieting Forever*, and the editor of *The Seven Spiritual Laws of Success* by Deepak Chopra, an international bestseller with over two million copies in print. Her life's mission is to publish books of enduring beauty, integrity, and wisdom, and to inspire others to fulfill their most cherished dreams.